Securing a Retirement Income for Life

Strategies for Managing, Protecting and Preserving Your Wealth

Bill Griffith, Jr., CFP®

W.E. Griffith Publications

Washington, PA

Published by W.E. Griffith Publications

Cover Design by Jonathan Gullery

International Standard Book Number (ISBN) 0-9785506-0-9

This publication is designed to provide accurate and authoritative information in regard to the subject matter covered. It is sold with the understanding that neither the author nor the publisher is engaged in rendering legal, accounting, or other professional service. If legal advice or other professional assistance is required, the services of a competent professional person should be sought.

-From a declaration of Principles jointly adopted by a Committee of the American Bar Association and a Committee of Publishers.

This book is intended to provide general information regarding appropriate retirement and estate planning actions based on the tax rules and other applicable laws in effect at the time of this writing, which are subject to change due to IRS and Congressional policy moves. It is not intended to be a substitute for the advice of a qualified practitioner. The author and publisher shall have neither liability nor responsibility to any person or entity with respect to any loss or damage caused, or alleged to be caused, directly or indirectly by the information contained in this publication.

Printed in the United States of America
1st printing

The CFP® certification mark is owned by the Certified Financial Planner Board of Standards, Inc.

S&P 500® is a registered trademark of The McGraw-Hill Companies, Inc.

This book is available at a special quantity discount to use as a premium or for educational purposes. For more information, please email pam@wegriffith.com or call 724. 228.3440 or write to W.E. Griffith Publications, 1150 Washington Road, Suite 200, Washington, PA 15301.

This book is dedicated to my family
for giving me all the time it took to write
– time that really belonged to them.

Contents

Preface

A new day is dawning. A new retirement is on the horizon. Significant changes over the years will have profound implications on the retirement planning process. To address these changes, planning and preparation will require more complex, innovative and "dynamic strategies" to meet these challenges head on. Although there are many things about the future that we know, much remains unknown. For instance, we know that the number of retirees is set to double over the next 30 years according to the U.S. Census Bureau. In 2008, the leading edge of the "so called" baby boom generation – those born between 1946 and 1964 – will turn 62.[1] Overall, this is an enormous generation of some 78 million Americans. This represents approximately 26 percent of the U.S. population (projected January 1, 2006).[2] For those who make up this generation, what type of retirement can they expect to have? A survey by the Certified Financial Planner Board of Standards, Inc. shows that 42 percent of high-income consumers fret about financial decisions and are not confident in their ability to control their financial future.[3]

Assumptions about the future are a crucial part of the retirement planning process. The investment needed to finance retirement depends on an accurate forecast of expenditures and rate of return assumptions well into the future. The uncertainty of traditional return assumptions is a significant risk in retirement, which can have a tremendous impact on retirement security.

Fewer retirees in the future can expect to receive a steady stream of income from employer provided defined benefit plans. This suggests that individuals will have to rely more on their own resources for a much higher percentage of their retirement income.

Surveys show that people are uncertain over whether Social Security will be there for them in the future. In 1945, there were 42 active workers for each retiree. Today, there are only three (3.3) workers for each retiree and this number is expected to fall to two (2.1) workers by 2031.[4] Even though Americans are unsure about the future of Social Security, the percentage of all workers who regularly save for retirement has dropped to 42%, the lowest rate since 1980.[5]

This book will provide answers to questions about:

- How much you will need to accumulate to provide a retirement income.

- What to do and how to go about planning to meet your retirement needs and objectives.

- How best to prepare for uncertainties in a world where the future is unknown.

- How long you can expect to live in retirement.

- How to implement the very best strategies for managing, protecting and preserving your wealth.

Retirement life in the future will be much different than in the past. For one thing, life in retirement will be much longer. For many people, retirement may represent the longest stage of their life. It is a time when they can look forward to a whole new range of exciting challenges and activities – to experience their own vision – with the same passion, excitement and sense of accomplishment they had during the first part of their life. Along with a much longer life, however, comes more complex and probably much more expensive financial challenges. This book will help you prepare for the many challenges and uncertainties that lie ahead as you approach retirement and during your retirement years.

In response to the changing paradigm surrounding the risks of funding future financial obligations, individuals have been forced to shoulder more of the financial burden. The shift away from defined benefit plans to defined contribution plans is a trend that has revolutionized retirement planning by placing more of the responsibility for saving on the individual. In 2005, 42% of all workers participated in defined contribution plans for pension coverage, up from 36% in 1999. In 2005, 21% of employees were in defined benefit plans.[6] Now more than ever, people are faced with having to make serious decisions about how to manage their company retirement plan, how much to contribute, how to invest their money and what to do with their vested balance after they retire. They need to have a plan based on clear and accurate information to help them make decisions about when to retire, how long they can expect to live in retirement and how much they need to accumulate.

Retirement planning isn't easy and the reality of successful investing is that it is a complicated and time-consuming process. Statistics show that 74% of people nearing retirement would prefer to consult with a professional financial advisor for reliable advice on retirement planning decisions.[7] The increasing number of people seeking financial advice to help them plan for retirement suggests that they are serious about achieving their goal. In fact, studies examining the retirement savings of baby boomers show that obtaining more education and guidance, like that provided in this book, are important factors contributing to larger amounts saved for retirement. A qualified professional can assist with the calculation of the accumulations needed to provide an income over an expected retirement lifetime. Through further analysis, a planner can determine the amount of additional money, if any, one would need to save through personal investments to reach that amount.

Meeting financial obligations through an investment-based approach, however, is only part of the process. Decisions about when to retire, how long you can expect to live in retirement and how much you need to accumulate are complicated by an ever changing set of circumstances. Throughout this book, we emphasize a process-driven approach for facing many of these and other critical issues in retirement. The interactive nature of this book will enable you to set more realistic goals based on accurate forecasts of cost and return assumptions in the future and protect against the risk of funding long-term liabilities by sharing the risk of financial burdens. In light of the anticipated challenges in retirement, a more acceptable approach is to use a combination of methods designed to increase the likelihood of achieving your goal of financial freedom.

References

[1] U.S. Census Bureau.

[2] Authors calculations based on U.S. Census Bureau projections for 2006.

[3] Certified Financial Planner Board of Standards, Inc. Consumer Survey.

[4] Social Security Administration.

[5] Roper ASW.

[6] U.S. Department of Labor; Bureau of Labor Statistics.

[7] ING – Business Journal; Baby Boomers Not Getting the Retirement Message.

Chapter 1

Planning a Retirement Income for Life

"If you can see yourself in possession of your goal,
it's half yours." – Tom Hopkins

H ow would you like to be financially independent with a retirement income for life? The goal of financial security during retirement is the subject of this chapter. The material in this chapter is fundamental to the process of building a secure retirement income for life. The process of building financial security requires a commitment to managing your investments in a way that will enable you to achieve your goal. The strategies that you learn in this book will give you the tools and confidence you need to be successful.

Planning and preparation is the key to achieving financial freedom. Do you dream about your vision of retirement? Do you think about the type of lifestyle you will have? Would you like to travel the world, start a new business, support your children in their endeavors or write a book about your life? How do you feel about your present financial situation? Are you excited about the prospect of achieving financial freedom and security? Are you on track financially? Are you confident in your ability to achieve your dreams? Do you have a plan for achieving them? Do you share in the realization that by coordinating and managing today's financial decisions, you can achieve your goals for tomorrow?

Developing A Plan

The very first step in the process of achieving financial independence is the establishment of a clear goal in time and dollar specificity. In our practice, we believe that our clients must set their own goals. We also believe it is our responsibility to educate them in defining and quantifying their goals. Since thoughts without action are only dreams, you need to quantify your thoughts and develop a plan to maximize the success of achieving them. Get excited about your retirement income goal. Try to visualize what it will mean to you and your family. Retirement isn't only about money. Think about the lifestyle you plan to have. What do you want to do when you retire? Retirement can be one of the most fulfilling times of your life if you plan for it properly. The more you plan, the better prepared you will be for the transition into your new lifestyle. Building an investment portfolio will provide you with the wealth needed to enjoy financial freedom and the time to fulfill many of your life dreams. It can be a time of renewal. Can you see yourself in possession of your goal?

The most successful way to make the transition to retirement is by planning what you will do. Take some time right now to answer the following questions and plan your personal future. List some of the things that you would like do during retirement.

Sports

_____

_____

_____

_____

Hobbies

_____

_____

_____

_____

Business Ventures

_____

_____

_____

_____

Volunteer Activities

_____

_____

_____

_____

Social Organizations

_____

_____

_____

_____

Have you defined your retirement income goal in a quantifiable dollar amount? Have you established a realistic time frame? If not, do it now. As you read through this chapter, make sure that the goals you establish are very specific. For example, suppose you want to receive an income of $100,000 each year for the length of your retirement life. How long do you plan on living after retirement? The initial amount needed to provide you with this income depends on, among other things, your existing resources, estimated years in retirement, the number of years until retirement and your risk tolerance level.

What is your age? _____ Spouse? _____

When do you want to be financially independent (how many years from now)? _____ Spouse? _____

How old will you be then? _____ Spouse? _____

What do you want your annual income to be? _____

Setting your goals will help you get clear about exactly what it is that you want to achieve. For example, suppose you are 45 years old today and you want to be financially independent in 15 years at the age of 60. What amount of income will allow you to do what you want to do? The object of answering these questions is to help you establish a more specific goal in terms of time and dollar specificity. How long do you want your income to last? Ten, twenty, thirty years or more? At the age of 60, one individual may project their lifespan to be only ten years. Another person may project twenty or thirty years or more. What is your lifespan? What if you are wrong? What if you run out of life with too much money left? Or, what if you run out of money with too much life left? The most significant transformation over the last 100 years has been an increase in longevity. Retirement may represent the longest stage of a person's life. Since people will be spending increasingly longer periods in retirement, the challenge is to assure that one never outlives their money, especially for basic living and healthcare expenses.

Have you ever tried to determine how much you will need to accumulate to provide your retirement income? Do you know what kind of investment portfolio you will need to last for your lifetime? The first thing you should do is to gather your latest bank, brokerage and investment company statements including all of your retirement and non-retirement accounts and complete the following worksheet (see Exhibit 1-1).

What is the combined value of all those assets earmarked for retirement? _____

EXHIBIT 1-1

RETIREMENT ACCUMULATIONS			
ASSETS	Assets titled in own name	Assets titled in spouses name	Assets titled jointly	Total Assets
Cash/Cash Equivalents	$_____	$_____	$_____	$_____
Annuities & Fixed Income Securities	$_____	$_____	$_____	$_____
Investments:				
Common Stocks	$_____	$_____	$_____	$_____
	$_____	$_____	$_____	$_____
	$_____	$_____	$_____	$_____
Mutual Funds	$_____	$_____	$_____	$_____
	$_____	$_____	$_____	$_____
	$_____	$_____	$_____	$_____
	$_____	$_____	$_____	$_____
Options, Commodities & Collectibles	$_____	$_____	$_____	$_____
	$_____	$_____	$_____	$_____
	$_____	$_____	$_____	$_____
Royalties & Mineral Interests	$_____	$_____	$_____	$_____
	$_____	$_____	$_____	$_____
	$_____	$_____	$_____	$_____
Other Investments	$_____	$_____	$_____	$_____
	$_____	$_____	$_____	$_____
	$_____	$_____	$_____	$_____
	$_____	$_____	$_____	$_____
Retirement Plans:				
Qualified Plans	$_____	$_____	$_____	$_____
	$_____	$_____	$_____	$_____
	$_____	$_____	$_____	$_____
	$_____	$_____	$_____	$_____
IRA's	$_____	$_____	$_____	$_____
	$_____	$_____	$_____	$_____
	$_____	$_____	$_____	$_____
	$_____	$_____	$_____	$_____
Closely Held Business Interest(s)	$_____	$_____	$_____	$_____
	$_____	$_____	$_____	$_____
	$_____	$_____	$_____	$_____
Real Estate	$_____	$_____	$_____	$_____
	$_____	$_____	$_____	$_____
	$_____	$_____	$_____	$_____
	$_____	$_____	$_____	$_____
Notes Receivable	$_____	$_____	$_____	$_____
	$_____	$_____	$_____	$_____
TOTALS	$	$	$	$

This book is about achieving a retirement income goal through savings and investing. You will learn about structuring investments in a way that enables one to meet significant goals. The way assets are allocated among the major classes of stocks, bonds, real estate and cash, consistent with ones tolerance for risk is known as the portfolio policy. In our firm, we believe that the portfolio policy is a significant determinant of long-term portfolio performance. Long-term portfolio performance is an important part of the retirement planning process.

What is the allocation of the assets (in stocks, bonds and cash) in your portfolio? _____

What is your risk profile? _____

Is the allocation of your investment portfolio appropriate for your risk profile? _____

What is your investment portfolios rate of return? _____

Are your assumptions realistic? Are you too conservative? Are your return requirements based on real rates of return?

If you want to achieve your goal of financial independence and freedom for tomorrow, you must be committed to managing and coordinating your financial decisions today. The time and effort you spend on setting your goals and developing a plan is crucial for success!

Overcoming the Obstacles

Research performed by the Employee Benefit Research Institute (EBRI) indicates that while people are aware of the need for planning, this awareness has not translated into action. Here are some of the reasons why people may not define and quantify their goals and develop a plan for achieving them:

1) The process may be considered too difficult.

2) Not knowing how to get started.

3) Procrastination.

4) No sense of urgency.

Whatever the reason, becoming financially independent will require a long-term commitment on your part. In many cases, it takes a substantial investment portfolio to support a financially independent lifestyle. As such, you cannot approach this kind of challenge half-heartedly. Those individuals who become financially independent typically are obsessed with goal setting and obtaining wealth!

1) They have clearly defined goals in time and dollar specificity.

2) They can visualize what achieving their goals will mean to them and their family.

3) They get excited about their goals and this excitement leads to action.

4) They remain focused and hold themselves responsible for their future.

5) They have a sense of urgency for achieving their goals.

The more reasons they have for achieving their retirement income goal, the more likely it is that they will remain focused on their plan of action. Now that you have established a more specific long-term retirement goal, state your reasons for becoming financially independent:

1) _____

2) _____

3) _____

4) _____

5) _____

6) _____

Your reasons for becoming financially independent will motivate you much more so than one big dollar amount. Along with planning and preparation, you must be determined to follow through. You should be thinking about what that large dollar amount will mean for you and your family. When I first sat down to write this book, I had so many important reasons to get my message out to people – to help them achieve their dreams, to make them aware of the risks in retirement and to help them confront these challenges. I was so focused on the reasons for achieving my goal that I did not even think about how long it would take and how difficult it would be to write this book. Every day, all I could think about was helping people live out their lives with financial freedom and independence.

Write Your Goals Down

If the time frame for achieving your retirement income goal is more than fifteen or twenty years away, you will need to set mid-term and short-term goals. The reason is simple. It can be overwhelming to think about the large amount of money you need to accumulate over a very long period of time. For example, if you compare what you will need in thirty or forty years to what you have right now, it may seem unattainable. In June 2000, my family and I were invited to a wedding in Lake Tahoe, Nevada. Actually, I was asked to be in the wedding. My first thought right after I opened the invitation was that we would not be able to go. I am from Pittsburgh and Lake Tahoe is 2400 miles away on the other side of the country. After awhile, the thought of going to Lake Tahoe seemed exciting. But driving the whole way out there by car was certainly out of the question. My children were still in school and the trip would definitely take at least two weeks out and back. I also thought about flying. We would get there a lot faster and the overall trip would take less time. But then I started to think about all the things we would miss seeing along the way in going from Pittsburgh to Nevada by plane. You cannot see much from 30,000 feet. But when you look at a map of the entire United States, the trip by car looked overwhelming - until I started to think about all the sights we could see and all of the wonderful things my family could experience along the way. Instead of taking the direct route out west, I thought about stops we could make along the way to see Mt. Rushmore and the Black Hills of South Dakota, the Rocky Mountains and Yellowstone National Park in Montana. After the wedding in Lake Tahoe, we could spend a night or two in Las Vegas and then stop to see the Hoover Dam on our way to the Grand Canyon in Arizona. I went right to the store and bought a trip planning software program. As it turned out, the actual fun was in planning the trip. It all started by thinking about how this could be a once in a lifetime opportunity to see all of these spectacular destinations with my family. I completely forgot about how many miles the trip was and how long it would take us to get there and back. Each stop along the way was an exciting destination in and of itself. It was an educational experience as well, especially for my two sons (ages nine and five at the time). Since we were always looking forward to the next stop along the way, we were actually in no hurry to get to Lake Tahoe. We drove an easy seven or eight hours each day. I cannot put into words how much I enjoyed my trip out west with my family. It was a once in a lifetime experience for all of us. I would do it all over again in a heartbeat. Although it was a long trip all the way out to our ultimate destination, the real joy was in the journey. Each step along the way was a once in a lifetime experience full of lessons learned. Each segment of our trip was worth so much more than just going from point A to point B. As an alternative, we could have decided to plan the quickest route straight across the country. After driving for seven or eight hours the first day, a quick look at the map would show that we still had about three-fourths of the trip left to go. Looking at it this way, the distance remaining in our trip could appear overwhelming. It would have been easy for us, at this point, to turn around and drive all the way back to Pittsburgh and either stay home or book the next available flight to Nevada. Can you see where I am going with this? If you think about it the right way and break your trip down into shorter destinations (goals) or in the case of planning for retirement - shorter-term objectives, you will discover that the real joy is in the journey. You will learn so much about yourself and your goals and your plan along the way. It is priceless! My trip out west was a significant accomplishment and a significant experience in my life. Financial freedom may in fact be one of the most significant goals in your life. Depending on your time frame, you may decide to set a five-year goal, a ten-year goal and a fifteen-year goal. If your time frame is longer, you could add a twenty, twenty-five or thirty year target. To be effective, you must write your goals down and then describe the steps you must take to accomplish them within each time period. Take some time right now to list your goals along with the steps you plan to take to achieve them. Better yet, start with a separate sheet of paper and a binder. In our firm, we give our clients a binder with, among other things, tabbed dividers to organize their important plans and documents. You can do the same thing. You should implement a system for planning, recording, organizing and tracking your progress.

Long-Term Retirement Objectives

Total Dollar Amount Needed   Time Frame

$_____   _____

Action Plan

_____

_____

_____

_____

_____

Mid-Term Objectives

Total Dollar Amount Needed   Time Frame

$_____   _____

Action Plan

_____

_____

_____

_____

_____

Mid-Term Objectives

Total Dollar Amount Needed   Time Frame

$_____   _____

Action Plan

_____

_____

_____

_____

_____

Mid-Term Objectives

Total Dollar Amount Needed   Time Frame

$_____   _____

Action Plan

_____

_____

_____

_____

_____

Mid-Term Objectives

Total Dollar Amount Needed   Time Frame

$_____   _____

Action Plan

_____

_____

_____

_____

_____

Short-Term Objectives

Total Dollar Amount Needed   Time Frame

$_____   _____

Action Plan

_____

_____

_____

_____

_____

Keep your goals in mind constantly as you read through this book. Your goals and the steps you plan to take to achieve them is work in progress. Make revisions in your work as your learn. Nothing is perfect the first time. Discuss your goals and action plans with your spouse. Work together and hold each other accountable. If you are committed to achieving financial freedom, setting goals and reducing them to writing is absolutely essential.

In the next chapter, we'll discuss the design and implementation of a plan to help you reach your goal based on where you are today.

Summary

Here is what you should hope to accomplish by reading this chapter:

The first step to achieving financial independence is to go through the process described in this chapter to establish your goal in time and dollar specificity.

The second part of the process described in this chapter is to gather and review your financial data.

The third part of the process is to write your goals down along with the steps you plan to take to achieve them.

Chapter Notes

Chapter 2

A Better Path to Financial Independence

"If you don't know where you're going, you'll probably end up somewhere else." – David Campbell

You too can become financially independent. It all starts with a plan. In Chapter 1, we discussed your goals. You must be absolutely passionate about your goals and dreams. To achieve your goals, you must establish a plan. Successful planning requires a well thought out process and discipline. This book provides a framework for getting there. We will help you remain focused on your long-term objectives by helping you implement a plan that takes into account many of life's uncertainties.

To truly become successful in planning a lifetime income, you must understand the challenges that lurk over the horizon and implement the very best strategies to meet those challenges head on. The challenges you face will depend on whether you are in the accumulation and protection stage or the income distribution and wealth preservation stage of your life.

The questions you answered in Chapter 1 regarding your current age, when you want to be financially independent and the income you want to receive will help determine your current needs and whether the focus should be on accumulation and protection or income distribution and wealth preservation (see Exhibit 2-1).

EXHIBIT 2-1

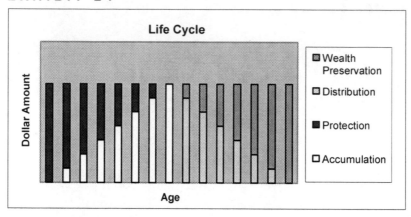

Which Side Of The Line Are You On?

If you are between the ages of 35 and 65, you will most likely be in the accumulation and protection phase where money that you save is invested and your investments are managed to increase in value during the first half of your life cycle. If you are over the age of 65, you will most likely be in the income distribution and preservation phase where money in your investment portfolio is distributed and your investments are managed to maintain your standard of living in the second half of your life cycle. One thing you will notice from the Life Cycle illustration is how the accumulations should grow over the years if properly managed. At younger ages, the accumulations are small and the need for protection is high. In the second half of the life cycle, accumulations decline as money in the investment portfolio is distributed. Advanced wealth strategies can also be used in the second half to preserve and enhance the value of ones estate. The horizontal line extends from one end to the other illustrating the need for an estate throughout ones life. The dollar amount required depends on individual circumstances. You should assess your own need for protection based on your age and the ages of your dependents (if any), your income, your financial obligations and the value of your asset base. In the second half of the life cycle, you should assess your need for advanced wealth preservation strategies. The most appropriate assets to own all depends on the challenges that you are likely to face in each phase. Some assets provide a more acceptable means of achieving a particular goal than others. What assets do you own and how can they help you achieve your goals?

Where Are You Now?

Before considering different strategies, you must complete a Financial Analysis Worksheet to determine your current financial position. Once again, refer to your latest bank, brokerage and investment company statements including all of your retirement and non-retirement accounts. This time, you will want to include the values of real estate and insurance (see Exhibit 2-2). The values contained on this worksheet should be correct as of a specific date and updated periodically over time. If you use a personal finance computer software program, it should be easy for you to produce a similar type of report.

What Is Your Income Goal?

The following Budget Worksheet is designed to assist you in establishing your retirement income goal (see Exhibit 2-3). Much of the information can be found in your check register. If you use a computer program, a similar report can be produced. All of this information will give you a clearer picture of where you stand financially. The Financial Analysis Worksheet will show you the value of your estate and how much you have saved already. The Annual Budget Worksheet will show how you spend your money. With more detailed information about your financial situation and a more specific goal in time and dollar specificity, you can begin to develop a plan that will make the best use of your current resources.

E X H I B I T   2-2

Financial Analysis Worksheet

CASH & SAVINGS
Checking Accounts	$_____
Savings Accounts	$_____
Money Market Accounts	$_____
CD's	$_____
Treasury Bills	$_____

INVESTMENTS
Mutual Funds	$_____
Stocks	$_____
Bonds	$_____
Annuities	$_____
Gold & Silver	$_____
TOTAL (a)	$_____

RETIREMENT PLANS
IRA's	$_____
SEP's	$_____
401(k) Plans	$_____
Profit Sharing Plans	$_____
Pension Plans	$_____
Other	$_____
TOTAL (b)	$_____

OTHER ASSETS
Business Interests	$_____
Limited Partnerships	$_____
Notes Receivable	$_____
Trust Deeds	$_____
Other	$_____
	$_____
TOTAL (c)	$_____

REAL ESTATE
	Market Value	-	Debt	=	Equity
Personal Residence	$_____		$_____		$_____
Vacation Home	$_____		$_____		$_____
Investment Property	$_____		$_____		$_____
Personal Property	$_____		$_____		$_____
			TOTAL Equity (d)		$_____

LIFE INSURANCE
	Face Value	Cash Value
Husband- Business	$_____	
Other	$_____	$_____
Wife- Business	$_____	
Other	$_____	$_____

TOTAL Insurance (f) $_____

Cash Value (e) $_____

TOTAL NET WORTH (a + b + c + d + e)	$_____
TOTAL Life Insurance (Face Value) (f)	$_____
TOTAL Net Worth PLUS Life Insurance	$_____

EXHIBIT 2-3

```
                        ANNUAL BUDGET WOKSHEET


Annual Expenditures                     Annual Receipts

Food                       $_____   Wages or salary                    $_____

Rent or mortgage payment(s) $_____  Interest (CD's, savings account, etc) $_____

Child care                 $_____   Dividends (mutual funds, stocks, etc.) $_____

Utilities                  $_____   Other                              $_____

Household maintenance      $_____                                      $_____

Savings                    $_____                                      $_____

Investing                  $_____                                  +   $_____

Retirement plan contributions $_____       Total Annual Receipts  $_____

Auto loan payment(s)       $_____

Auto maintenance           $_____

Transportation (gas, fares) $_____   Net Cash Flow

Income and Social Security taxes $_____  Total Annual Receipts         $_____

Property Taxes             $_____   Total Annual Expenditures      -   $_____

Clothing                   $_____

Insurance                  $_____           Annual Net Cash Flow  $_____

Credit card payments       $_____

Contributions              $_____

Entertainment              $_____

Charities                  $_____

Dues                       $_____

Other                  +   $_____

       Total Annual Expenditures  $_____
```

Where Do You Want To Go?

Successful planning requires a well thought out process and discipline. Without direction and discipline, you may end up with an array of investments, various kinds of insurance and other assets that may not fit together in a way that will help you achieve your goals. Worse yet, some assets may actually conflict with one another and interfere with your ability to achieve your goals. A better strategy is to integrate your retirement assets with other aspects of your financial situation such as insurance, tax issues and your estate plan. Rather than buying investments at random, a well defined portfolio with assets that all work together is a much better path to financial independence. This multidisciplinary approach to planning is a lifetime process running from one end of the life cycle to the other. It recognizes that your needs in the accumulation and protection phase of the life cycle are all interconnected. Likewise, your needs in the income distribution and wealth preservation phase in the second half of the life cycle are also interconnected. A systematic, multidisciplinary approach is a much more acceptable means of facing challenges on both sides of the line.

What are the challenges and how does a multidisciplinary approach work?

The following hypothetical scenarios show how the financial issues for each household are all interconnected and how the most acceptable means for achieving a goal is by using a systematic, multidisciplinary approach. There are four different scenarios that illustrate some of the planning principles discussed in later chapters. In each case there is an abbreviated version of a balance sheet and income statement. Other information for each scenario, retirement goals, highlights of the economy, assumptions and a brief analysis are all geared toward the subject of this book, which is securing a retirement income for life. The suggestions in each case are intended to provide general information regarding appropriate planning actions for different situations. The scenarios do not cover other goals, which may have a significant impact on planning decisions, such as college planning or comprehensive risk management. As you review these scenarios, you will see how retirement, estate planning, insurance and tax issues are all interconnected.

Scenario One

Husband	James DeWalt, 46
Wife	Beth DeWalt, 47
Children	Burke DeWalt, age 15
	Cara DeWalt, age 12

Financial Data from Balance Sheet

Cash (titled jointly)	$70,000
Stock in ABC Corporation (James)	$175,000
Retirement Plans	
401(k) –James	$320,000
IRA –Beth	$250,000
Personal Residence (titled jointly)	$350,000

Financial Data from Income Statement

Salary – James	$100,000
Salary – Beth	$65,000
Interest Income	$2,100
Core living expenses & taxes	$148,500

Other Information

They are in the 31% marginal tax bracket (state and federal combined).

The cash is invested in a money market fund.

The 401(k) is invested in money market mutual funds.

The IRA is invested in money market mutual funds.

The tax basis of their residence is $165,000; and the stock is $100,000.

They currently save $18,600 per year for retirement.

They consider themselves to be knowledgeable investors with a moderate tolerance for risk.

They each own term life insurance policies with a $250,000 death benefit on each. Their children are contingent beneficiaries.

They have no estate planning documents.

Retirement Goal

Retirement in 20 years with an income from their retirement plans and personal investments.

Highlights of the US Economy

The US economy continued to grow at a strong pace. The Consumer Price Index (CPI) rose a modest 3.40% for the year.

Assumptions Going Forward

Annual increase in CPI	3.00%
Projected return on:	
S&P 500®	10.73%
International Equity	7.56%
Fixed Income	6.24%

Analysis

Their current portfolio is positioned as conservative and contains excessive purchasing power and company risk. Their existing holdings do not coincide with their assessment of themselves as moderate investors. A moderate risk profile would result in a diversified portfolio with an after-tax return of 6.64%. If their current portfolio of $815,000 is repositioned as they continue to save $18,600 per year for retirement in 20 years, the ending portfolio value will be approximately $3,681,425. To maintain their standard of living in retirement, their income would be approximately $268,000 per year. A withdrawal of $268,000 at the beginning of each year (adjusted for inflation) would totally deplete their portfolio in roughly 19 years. There is a high probability that they will outlive their money if their joint life expectancy exceeds 19 years.

On the protection side, they are both underinsured. If James dies prematurely, the $250,000 death benefit may replace his income for a period of only 7 years. If Beth dies prematurely, the $250,000 death benefit may replace her income for a period of only 14 years. If they both die prematurely, their total estate of approximately $1,665,000 would not be of any help to their children without the appropriate estate documents since proceeds from life insurance policies and retirement plans cannot be paid out to minors.

Based on this scenario, James and Beth need to address issues related to protection for each other and their children by evaluating their life insurance and estate plan. Additionally, they should reposition their portfolio to reduce or eliminate the purchasing power and company risk. They should also address the risk of outliving their money.

Scenario Two

Husband	Jeffrey Williams, 54 year old physician
Wife	Kathy Williams, 52 self-employed accountant
Children	Brad Williams, age 16
	Tiffany Williams, age 14

Financial Data from Balance Sheet

Cash (titled jointly)	$350,000
Single premium deferred annuity (Jeffrey)	$275,000
Single premium deferred annuity (Kathy)	$150,000
Insurance cash value (Jeffrey)	$50,000
Insurance cash value (Kathy)	$35,000
Stocks in four high tech companies (Jeffrey)	$450,000
Retirement Plans	
Qualified plan – Jeffrey	$1,500,000
Qualified plan – Kathy	$900,000
Real Estate	
Office building (titled jointly)	$1,500,000
Personal residence (titled jointly)	$1,200,000
Vacation home – out of state (titled jointly)	$650,000
Automobiles (Jeffrey)	$135,000
Personal property (titled jointly)	$240,000

Financial Data from Income Statement

Salary – Jeffrey	$230,000
Salary – Kathy	$125,000
Interest Income	$21,000
Rental income	$18,000
Core living expenses & taxes	$315,000

Other Information

They are in the 39% marginal tax bracket (state and federal combined).

The cash is invested in a money market fund.

The qualified plans are invested in growth mutual funds; Kathy is the beneficiary of Jeffrey's plan and Jeffrey is the beneficiary of Kathy's plan. The children are equal contingent beneficiaries.

The tax basis of their residence is $600,000; and the stock is $100,000.

They currently save $79,000 per year for retirement.

They consider themselves to be aggressive investors with no need for current income.

They each own universal life insurance policies with a $500,000 death benefit on each. Their children are contingent beneficiaries.

Jeffrey's medical practice is a corporation and Kathy operates as a sole proprietor.

They spend several weeks in their vacation home throughout the year. Since their son recently got a summer job, he frequently stays home when the family goes away.

They have simple wills; Jeffrey leaves his estate to Kathy and Kathy leaves her estate to Jeffrey.

Retirement Goal

Jeffrey and Kathy both want to retire in 11 years. They would like to be able to spend $25,000 (after taxes) per month in today's dollars during retirement.

Highlights of the US Economy

The US economy grew at a modest rate. The Consumer Price Index (CPI) rose a modest 2.8% for the year.

Assumptions Going Forward

Annual increase in CPI	4.00%
Projected return on:	
S&P 500®	13.90%
International Equity	16.10%
Fixed Income	9.81%

Analysis

Excluding assets devoted to personal use, their current investment portfolio is approximately $3,625,000. The current portfolio is positioned as moderate and contains excessive purchasing power and company risk. Their existing holdings do not coincide with their assessment of themselves as aggressive. An aggressive risk profile would result in a diversified portfolio with an after-tax return of 8.63%. If their current portfolio is repositioned as they continue to save $79,000 per year for retirement in 11 years, the ending portfolio value will be approximately $10,371,000. To maintain their standard of living in retirement, their income would be approximately $462,000 per year. After repositioning their portfolio, a withdrawal rate of 4.5% should sustain this portfolio for the rest of their lives. Although there is a high probability that they will not outlive their money, there are other risks that may threaten their financial future.

On the protection side, they each have $500,000 life insurance policies. If Jeffrey dies prematurely, the $500,000 death benefit may replace his income for a period of only 4 years. If Kathy dies prematurely, her $500,000 death benefit may replace her income for a period of only 13 years. If they both die prematurely, their total estate of approximately $7,435,000 would not be of any help to their children without the appropriate estate documents since proceeds from life insurance policies and retirement plans cannot be paid out to minors. Worse yet, without significant changes to their estate plan only one of their federal estate tax equivalent exemptions can be used to reduce their estate for federal estate tax purposes (the exclusion is $2,000,000 in 2006-2008). The remaining $5,435,000 is subject to estate tax at the marginal rate of 46% (in 2006 and 45% in 2007). The estate tax can be as high as $2,500,000! Roughly one half of their estate is in liquid non-retirement assets that could be used to pay these taxes. The other half is in qualified retirement plans. Total distributions from these accounts are subject to both estate and income taxation.

Also on the protection side, they both have significant exposure to liability risks. The form of ownership of Jeffrey's medical practice (corporation) and Kathy's accounting firm (sole proprietorship) provides very little asset protection. Additionally, their real estate and all other personal assets are not protected in the event of a lawsuit. If their 16-year old son drives the family car, there is a liability threat there as well. I am sure that their 16-year old son would never think of having friends over while his parents are away. Having any kind of party with alcohol is definitely out of the question. Right! In that case, there is no reason for them to worry about a carload of teenagers leaving their home under the influence. Wrong! Asset protection is the number one priority in this scenario. One bad accident could kill not only people but a great retirement plan as well! Based on a brief analysis of this scenario, Jeffrey and Kathy need to address issues related to asset protection immediately and then update their life insurance and estate plan as well to include advanced wealth preservation strategies. A team of experts is advised.

Scenario Three

Husband	Thomas Brown, 71 retired
Wife	Marilyn Brown, 70
Children	Kimberly Cox, age 47
	David Brown, age 41

Financial Data from Balance Sheet

Cash (titled jointly)	$49,000
Bank CD (Thomas)	$137,250
Bank CD (Marilyn)	$81,000
Stock in XYZ Corporation	$350,000
Retirement Plans	
Profit sharing plan – Thomas	$1,050,000
IRA – Marilyn	$50,000
Personal residence (titled jointly)	$350,000
Automobiles (Thomas)	$51,000
Personal property (titled jointly)	$100,000

Financial Data from Income Statement

Income – (combined)	$70,000
Interest income	$15,000
Dividend income	$13,500
Social Security income	$27,000
Core living expenses & taxes	$96,000

Other Information

They are in the 31% marginal tax bracket (state and federal combined).

The cash is invested in a money market fund.

The profit sharing plan is invested 75% in fixed income and 25% S&P 500®.

The IRA is invested in money market mutual funds.

Marilyn is the beneficiary of Tom's retirement plan and Tom is the beneficiary of Marilyn's plan. The children are equal contingent beneficiaries.

The tax basis of their residence is $105,000; and the stock is $100,000.

They currently reinvest $29,500 per year in bank money market accounts.

They consider themselves to be knowledgeable investors with a moderate risk tolerance level.

They do not have any life insurance or long-term care insurance. Both are in excellent health.

They have a revocable living trust, credit shelter trust, durable powers of attorney for healthcare and assets and pour-over wills.

Retirement Goal

Maintain their current standard of living including frequent travel out of state to visit their children. Revise their estate plan to minimize transfer taxes including federal, estate and income taxes. Maximize amounts passing to their children. Evaluate rollover options for retirement plan.

Highlights of the US Economy

The economic environment exhibits a low real return on cash. The US economy continued to show little signs of growth.

Assumptions Going Forward

Annual increase in CPI	2.00%
Projected return on:	
S&P 500®	2.09%
International Equity	7.00%
Fixed Income	5.91%

Analysis

Their current portfolio is positioned as stable and contains excessive purchasing power and company risk. Their existing holdings do not coincide with their assessment of themselves as moderate investors. A moderate risk profile would result in a diversified portfolio with a target rate of return of 2.3.%. Their current portfolio of $1,717,250 is providing a retirement income of approximately $98,500. To maintain their standard of living in retirement, their income would increase each year adjusted for inflation sustaining their portfolio for approximately 18 years. There is a high probability that they will outlive their money if their joint life expectancy exceeds 18 years.

On the protection side, neither one of them has long-term care insurance. The need for long-term health care could quickly drain their portfolio much sooner than expected. Their total estate of approximately $2,218,250 may not be subject to federal estate taxation (the exclusion is $2,000,000 in 2006-2008). Their estate plan should be reviewed periodically to determine the need for advanced planning (the exclusion amount goes down to $1,000,000 after 2010). The company plan may require a lump sum distribution resulting in significant income and estate tax consequences. In this case, an eligible rollover distribution should be considered.

Based on this scenario, Thomas and Marilyn should address issues related to health care. They should evaluate their need for advanced wealth preservation strategies in light of the uncertainty surrounding the repeal of the estate tax. Additionally, they should reposition their portfolio to reduce current income taxes while at the same time reducing the risk of outliving their money.

Scenario Four

Husband	Matthew Johnson, 65 Business Owner
Wife	Elizabeth Johnson, 63
Children	William Johnson, age 44
	Erin Brown, age 41
	Sandy Marshall, age 38

Financial Data from Balance Sheet

Cash (titled jointly)	$25,000
Life insurance cash value (Matthew)	$58,000
Stock in XYZ Corporation	$10,000
Retirement plans	
Roth IRA – Matthew	$30,000
Closely held business (titled jointly)	$1,500,000
Personal residence (titled jointly)	$250,000
Automobiles (Matthew)	$75,000
Personal property (titled jointly)	$150,000

Financial Data from Income Statement

Salary – Matthew	$75,000
Core living expenses & taxes	$75,000

Other Information

They are in the 28% marginal tax bracket (state and federal combined).

XYZ Corporation is a technology company.

The Roth IRA is invested 75% in equity and 25% in fixed income.

The tax basis of their business is $200,000.

The tax basis of their residence is $95,000; and the stock is $5,000.

Elizabeth is the beneficiary of Matthew's retirement plan and the children are equal contingent beneficiaries.

The tax basis of their residence is $105,000.

They consider themselves to be average investors with a moderate risk tolerance level.

Matthew has a $250,000 universal life insurance policy; Elizabeth does not have life insurance. They both have long-term care insurance. Both are in good health.

They have a revocable living trust, credit shelter trust, durable powers of attorney for healthcare and assets and pour-over wills.

Retirement Goal

Transfer ownership of their business to their oldest son with minimal tax consequences. Their other children have no interest in the family business. Maintain their current standard of living including frequent travel out of state. Revise their estate plan to minimize transfer taxes including federal, estate and income taxes. Maximize amounts passing to their children.

Highlights of the US Economy

The economic environment exhibits a low real return on cash. The US economy shows signs of increased growth.

Assumptions Going Forward

Annual increase in CPI	3.00%
Projected return on:	
S&P 500®	18.33%
International Equity	9.21%
Fixed Income	8.14%

Analysis

Their current portfolio is positioned as conservative. Their current investment portfolio of $65,000 will not be a significant source of current income. By repositioning their portfolio, Matthew and/or his heirs can benefit from the tax-free growth and withdrawals with the Roth IRA. In addition, there are no required distributions with the Roth. Matthew and Elizabeth can freeze the value of their business for estate tax purposes, reduce capital gain exposure and transfers their business to their son using advanced wealth preservation strategies. In return, they could receive income payments for life. They should evaluate the need for the $250,000 universal life insurance policy owned by Matthew.

All four hypothetical scenarios show how the financial issues for each household are all interconnected and how the most acceptable means for achieving a goal is by using a systematic, multidisciplinary approach. As you study these scenarios, you will see how retirement, estate planning, insurance and tax issues are all interconnected. If the focus is entirely on one area, such as wealth accumulation, without regard to protection, an entire lifetime worth of saving and investing can be wiped out by one nasty lawsuit. Retirement and estate plans are not complete without protection against malpractice, errors and omissions and personal liability claims. And the larger the asset base, the greater the need for protection. Consider your own circumstances and the personal exposure to potential liability risks with the assets you own. All of your personal assets, such as your personal residence, vacation homes, automobiles, boats, off road vehicles, residential and commercial rental properties, investment accounts, bank accounts, collectibles and any other personal property and collectibles need protection. Most people have at least some insurance coverage to protect against personal liability. The problem is there is a limit as to the amount of protection provided via the insurance policy. In the course of reviewing asset protection needs, it is prudent for one to implement some form of asset protection program that protects against claims that could exceed insurance policy limits. The key is determining which asset protection strategies are most appropriate for each individual situation. In our analysis of scenario two (Jeffrey and Kathy Williams), we mentioned that they both have significant exposure to liability risks. The form of ownership of Jeffrey's medical practice (corporation) and Kathy's accounting firm (sole proprietorship) provides very little asset protection. Most people incorporate to limit their personal liability in the event of a claim against the corporation. With corporations that provide personal services, however, the personal liability is not removed by incorporating. A person can still be held personally liable. With Kathy's accounting firm as a sole proprietorship, she is personally liable for all actions of the business. Additionally, their real estate and all other personal assets are not protected in the event of a lawsuit. Many people think that a $1 million umbrella policy will protect them if they get sued for negligence. If someone leaves their home after drinking alcohol and is involved in an accident causing serious injury or death to others, a $1 million dollar insurance policy will provide little protection. Their personal assets are at risks if a claim exceeds $1 million. Based on a brief analysis of their situation, Jeffrey and Kathy need to address issues related to asset protection immediately and coordinate those issues with other aspects of their financial and estate plan. Once again, a team of experts is advised.

There are many asset protection strategies that include the use of trusts, such as domestic and offshore trusts. Converting property to another form of ownership, such as a limited liability company and a family limited partnership is another strategy. As described above, choosing the right business entity is another important consideration for asset protection purposes. And although insurance provides limited protection, due to the policy limits described above, almost everyone needs some form of insurance to provide a base of protection.

Family Limited Partnership

A family limited partnership (FLP) is a legal entity in which the family members are partners. Essentially, family members transfer assets into an FLP. The FLP then owns the assets. In exchange for these assets, partners receive an interest in the FLP. In the typical arrangement, a parent is the general partner and the children are limited partners. The general partner may hold only a one or two percent interest in the partnership while the limited partners hold the remaining 98% to 99%. What makes the FLP appropriate from an asset protection standpoint is that, since the general partners no longer own the assets (transferred into the FLP), the assets are protected if the general partners are sued even though as general partners, they still retain control of the assets transferred into the FLP. The lack of control and marketability over the interests owned by limited partners produces discounted values. As such, FLP's provide ancillary benefits for estate tax purposes. It is important to know that there are restrictions as to the types of assets that can be transferred into a family limited partnership. Additionally, FLP's must be set up properly. Anyone interested in the establishment of an FLP should do so with the oversight of an experienced practitioner.

Limited Liability Company

A limited liability company provides for the pass-through of income for tax purposes, similar to a partnership, and for liability protection, similar to that of a corporation. It combines the best of both worlds. Unlike a family limited partnership, many other types of assets can be held in LLC's. For example, personal property and other assets with relatively low values can be placed in an LLC. Although certain assets may not be worth very much, they can represent an enormous potential liability risk (i.e. a boat, off-road vehicle, etc.). In contrast to a corporation, however, LLC's typically provide more asset protection than corporations where personal services are offered.

While these scenarios and many others show how unanticipated events could potentially impact retirement portfolios, you should understand that over the long term, in good times and bad, you need to remain focused on an integrated, multidisciplinary approach to meeting their goals and objectives.

In the next chapter, we will introduce three risks that people face in retirement and how successful planning takes into account these uncertainties in life.

Summary

Successful planning requires a well thought out process and discipline.

To truly become successful in planning a lifetime income, you must understand the challenges that lurk over the horizon and implement the very best strategies to meet those challenges head on.

You need to know where you stand financially in order to develop a plan that will make the best use of your current resources.

A systematic, multidisciplinary approach to planning recognizes that your needs are all interconnected in both phases of the life cycle.

Chapter Notes

Chapter 3

Risks in Retirement

"There are two times in a mans life when he
should not speculate: when he can't afford it
and when he can." - Mark Twain

I n the previous chapter, we showed how unanticipated events
could potentially impact retirement portfolios. To truly become
successful in planning a lifetime income, you must understand
the challenges that lurk over the horizon and implement the very best
strategies to meet those challenges head on.

In this chapter, we will introduce three risks that people face in
retirement:

> ➢ The Market Risk
> ➢ The Risk of Not Saving Enough
> ➢ The Longevity Risk

All three have one thing in common – uncertainty. Successful planning today requires more complex, innovative and dynamic financial
solutions for managing this uncertainty. You can no longer rely on
one single solution. Since so much about the future is unknown,
the best you can do in many cases is to make an educated guess about
what may happen. When you do this, however, you take the chance
of being right or wrong. In either case, the individual shoulders the
risk. With so much at stake, we believe a better solution is to share

the risk. Later in the book, we provide innovative and dynamic financial solutions to protect against the unknown by removing or shifting the risk away from the individual.

The Market Risk

Market risk refers to the possibility that your portfolio will lose value due to changing conditions in the capital markets. This fluctuation is referred to as volatility and the degree to which this fluctuation occurs is called the standard deviation. Although it is impossible to reduce risk completely, diversification can reduce the overall volatility of your portfolio. One of the advantages of diversification is that the performance of your portfolio will be less dependent on the return of one asset class. By investing in different asset classes with offsetting returns, you can attempt to protect your portfolio against major losses.

This uncertainty is compounded by the fact that you cannot predict when the next occurrence of an extended market decline or "bear market" will be. An extended market decline soon after retirement could jeopardize the sustainability of withdrawals over the life of the retirement period. Therefore, it is essential to make appropriate asset allocation decisions based on real rates of return rather than on a constant or so called "average rate of return."

As you will see later in the book, this uncertainty is much more of a risk for most people than the longevity risk.

The Risk of Not Saving Enough

In Chapter 2, we used hypothetical scenarios to show how four different households fare in their desire to achieve the goal of securing a retirement income for life. In at least two out of the four scenarios, the couples were at risk of outliving their money. This is despite the fact that they had existing portfolios and they were continuing to save for the future. One solution would be for each couple to examine the possibility of saving more. While most people know they can and should save more for retirement, studies show they are not doing so. A study conducted by Hewitt Associates, a global resources services firm, examined the saving and investing habits of *FORTUNE 500* company employees in conjunction with researchers from Harvard University and the Wharton School of the University of Pennsylvania.[1] What they found was that the majority of people surveyed were not saving enough for retirement. This is despite the fact that nearly three-quarters of the employees were aware that they should be saving at least two-to-three times as much as they currently were. Do you know how much more you should be saving for retirement?

Social Security, defined benefit plans and personal savings have traditionally provided the lion's share of a retiree's income. In the future, defined contribution plans and personal savings will become significantly more important sources of a retiree's income. Research shows that Americans express uncertainty over whether Social Security will be there for them in the future. In 1945, there were 42 active workers for each retiree. Today, there are only three workers for each retiree and this number is expected to fall to two workers by 2030.[2] Even though Americans are unsure about the future of Social Security, the percentage of all workers who regularly save for retirement has dropped to 42%, the lowest rate since 1980.[3] Although Social Security is expected to become less important as a source of income in the future, most would expect at least some part of their retirement income to come from Social Security at retirement age.

Do you know when you will be eligible for full Social Security benefits?

As you will see from the following table, the full-benefit retirement age, enacted in 1983, gradually increases ultimately to age 67 (see Exhibit 3-1).

EXHIBIT 3-1

The Social Security Full-Benefit Retirement Age, 2002-2025		
Year of Birth	Year You Will Reach Age 65	Full Benefit Age yrs./months
1937	2002	65
1938	2003	65/2
1939	2004	65/4
1940	2005	65/6
1941	2006	65/8
1942	2007	65/10
1943-1954	2008-2019	66
1955	2020	66/2
1956	2021	66/4
1957	2022	66/6
1958	2023	66/8
1959	2024	66/10
1960 and later	2025 and later	67

Source: Social Security Online
(http://www.ssa.gov.)

Are you uncertain over whether Social Security will be there for you in the future?

Social Security and company pension plans have customarily provided a large percentage of a retiree's total income. In 1998, 58 percent of households with at least one member age 65 depended on Social Security for 50 percent or more of their total income.[4] In the same year, one in four households depended on Social Security for more than 90 percent of their income. The number of active workers for each retiree has declined dramatically over the years. As stated earlier, there are only three workers for each retiree today and this number is expected to fall to two workers by 2031. Although it is hard to say how the benefits and eligibility requirements will change over the years, as long as there is a payroll tax, you would expect at least some "minimal benefits" from Social Security in the future. If Social Security can be expected to provide only minimal benefits in retirement, some people may choose to exclude Social Security benefits from retirement planning projections. Others may choose to consider both scenarios, with and without Social Security benefits.

Even with the uncertainty over Social Security, the percentage of all workers who regularly save for retirement has dropped to 42%, the lowest rate since 1980. In January 2006, the U.S. Commerce Department reported that the personal savings rate in America has dropped to negative numbers for the first time since the Great Depression at minus 0.5 percent, meaning that Americans not only spent all of their after-tax income in 2005, but they had to dip into previous savings or borrowing.

Do you know how much you will need to accumulate to provide a retirement income for life?

The shift away from defined benefit (DB) plans, in which workers receive a guaranteed retirement income, to defined contribution (DC) plans is a trend that has revolutionized retirement planning by placing more of the responsibility for saving on the individual. In 2005, 42% of all workers participated in defined contribution plans for pension coverage, up from 36% in 1999. In 2005, 21% of employees were in defined benefit plans. The move away from defined benefit plans is due in part to a decline in stock market returns leaving many plans under funded, which underscores the financial risk employers must undertake in providing DB plans. As the shift away from DB plans has been motivated by a desire to eliminate this type of financial risk, employees are assuming the financial risk of DC plans. Now more than ever, employees are faced with having to make serious decisions about how to manage their company retirement plan, how much to contribute, how to invest their money and what to do with their vested balance after they retire.

How much you will need to accumulate depends on the lifestyle you envision and the length of your retirement life. Do you expect to maintain your standard of living or enhance your standard of living? If you plan on having an active lifestyle after retirement that may include a new business venture, extensive travel schedule or an expensive recreational activity, you will need to account for this increase in your budget and in your retirement income calculations.

Once you have a retirement lifestyle in mind with the expected number of years in retirement, you can determine the amount of money needed to meet your needs. In Chapter 4, you will learn how to develop an investment strategy designed to achieve your goals. A qualified professional can also assist with the calculation of the accumulations needed to provide an income over an expected retirement lifetime. Through further analysis, a planner can help you determine the amount of additional money, if any, you would need to save through personal investments to reach that amount.

The Longevity Risk

As a nation we are living longer than ever before. In 1990, only 37,000 Americans were age 100 or older. In 2050, over one million Americans are projected to be 100 years of age or older.[5] There is a 40% chance of one person from a married couple age 60 reaching 95! This increase in longevity brings many new challenges to the retirement planning process. These new challenges will require knowledge about more advanced planning strategies to help you overcome abundant misperceptions and confront these new challenges head-on. How long do you hope to live? How long do you want your retirement income to last? Ten, twenty, thirty years? What are the chances that you will live to be 100 years of age or older? What if you are wrong? What if you outlive your money? If you worry about outliving your money, you may under-spend during retirement thus having a sub-optimal retirement. If you overspend during retirement, you may simply run out of money. One of the biggest mistakes one can make is to underestimate how long they are likely to live. As life expectancies continue to increase, people should plan on living for a very long time. You should never use simplified projections based on the average life expectancy of the typical retiree. As you will see later in this book, basing your retirement income projections on averages can be dangerous to your wealth. Instead, you should consider your own health status and your family history. Do you have longevity in your family? If so, maybe you should plan on the possibility of living to at least the age of 100.

Take a few minutes right now to contemplate your own retirement lifetime. How long do you expect to live in retirement? What about your spouse?

Summary

This book will help you prepare for the many challenges and uncertainties that lie ahead by confronting three risks in retirement: the market risk, the risk of not saving enough, and the longevity risk.

Now more than ever, you need a plan based on clear and accurate information to help you make decisions about when to retire, how long you can expect to live in retirement and how much you need to accumulate.

In light of the anticipated challenges in retirement, you will learn how to use a combination of multidisciplinary strategies to increase the likelihood of achieving your goal.

In the next chapter, we will discuss the critical issues in retirement income planning.

References

[1] Hewitt Associates LLC.
[2] Social Security Administration.
[3] Roper ASW.
[4] U.S. Department of Labor.
[5] U.S. Census Bureau, 2002.

Chapter 4

Critical Issues in Retirement Income Planning

"Inflation is when the buck doesn't stop anywhere."
- Anonymous

I n the last chapter, you learned about the market risk. Market risk refers to the possibility that your portfolio will lose value due to changes in market conditions. The degree to which your portfolio fluctuates in value is referred to as volatility. Although it is impossible to reduce market risk completely, diversification can reduce the overall volatility of your portfolio. In our firm, we believe in developing client-specific investment strategies that emphasize diversified asset allocation. Through that objective driven process, crucial factors such as appropriate levels of risk and return are derived and optimized to achieve specific objectives.

Asset Allocation

What is asset allocation? Asset allocation is the process of combining asset classes such as cash, stocks, and bonds in a portfolio in order to meet your goals (see Exhibit 4-1).

What is the best way to allocate your assets? In our practice, we allocate assets among the major asset classes of cash, stocks, bonds and real estate. Stocks are divided between domestic and foreign and

EXHIBIT 4-1

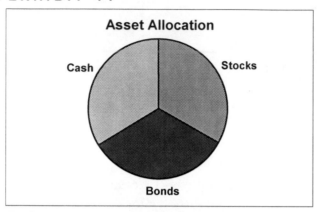

For illustrative purposes only and not indicative of any investment.

large and small capitalization. We further divide domestic stocks into growth and value styles. Bonds are divided by short, intermediate and long-term duration. We use real estate investment trusts (REITs) for the real estate component of the plan. There is no one particular investment strategy that is appropriate for all people. An investment plan should be based on each person's specific needs, circumstances and goals. The optimal plan will depend on the amount and timing of cash flow needs, tax considerations and market conditions. The financial decisions you make would be based, therefore, on your specific objectives. Your tolerance for risk and the length of your investment time horizon greatly affect the asset allocation decision. So the way in which your assets are allocated or diversified in varying proportions is one of the most important factors that determines both the risk and return of your portfolio. **The effect of the asset allocation decision far exceeds the effects of market timing or the specific securities that you invest in.**

The asset allocation of your investment portfolio can be designed after a target rate of return is established. Return requirements should be based on your specific tolerance for risk.

In Chapter 1, we asked you a question about your risk profile. Your answer to this question will lead to a portfolio closely aligned with your ability to accept risk and loss. At our firm, we ask our clients to complete a Risk Tolerance Questionnaire. After careful consideration of each of the responses to the questions, we can determine our client's appetite for risk and use it to determine which risk/return profile from Capital Preservation to Aggressive Growth matches their situation. Determining where you are in terms of risk and return establishes the foundation for moving forward to the next step.

What is your tolerance for risk? _____

There are two approaches to asset allocation. One is the strategic approach. The other is the tactical approach. In addition to the allocation of your assets, the manner in which your assets are periodically rebalanced is an important factor that can greatly reduce the volatility or risk of your portfolio over time. With a strategic allocation, your assets are rebalanced to the original target asset mix. With a tactical allocation, your assets are rebalanced within certain ranges based upon a more opportunistic view of the market or based upon changing economic conditions.

In Chapter 2, we asked you if the allocation of your investment portfolio is appropriate for your risk profile. We also asked you about your investment portfolios rate of return.

Putting It All Together

Now it is time to put all of your answers together. Based on your answers to the following questions, you will be able to develop an investment strategy designed to achieve your goals.

Time Horizon

What is your current age?_____ Spouse? _____

When do you want to be financially independent (how many years from now)? _____ Spouse? _____

How old will you be then? _____ Spouse? _____

What do you want your annual income to be?_____

How long do you hope to live? _____ Spouse?_____

Estimated number of years in retirement?_____

Investable Resources

What is the combined value of all those assets earmarked for retirement? _____

What is the allocation of these assets (in stocks, bonds and cash)?

Stocks_____%

Bonds _____%

Cash _____%

Tolerance For Risk

What is your risk profile? _____

Is the allocation of your investment portfolio appropriate for your risk profile? _____

What is your investment portfolio's rate of return? _____

There are a variety of ways to implement your investment strategy.

Based on your time horizon and tolerance for risk, you should:

- Develop a diversified portfolio based on a strategic or tactical allocation strategy.

- Select a domestic and/or global investment strategy.

- Exercise care in the appropriate placement of investments within taxable and tax-deferred accounts.

Why is this so important? First, since the definition of money is purchasing power, you will want to attempt to provide a hedge against inflation, especially in the distribution and preservation phase of your life. If you are in the accumulation and protection phase, you will want to attempt to provide a large enough investment portfolio to sustain you for the rest of your life, especially for your core living expenses.

The Consumer Price Index (CPI) is the most widely used measure of inflation (see Exhibit 4-2).

EXHIBIT 4-2

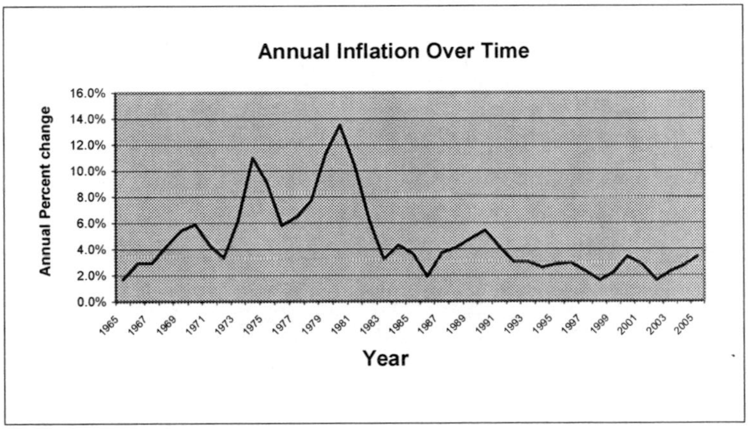

Source: U.S. Bureau of Labor Statistics

As you can see, changes in the Consumer Price Index (CPI) have been dramatic over the years. In the 1970s and early 80s, inflation rates were as high as 9.1%, 10.4%, 11%, 11.3% and 13.5%. In the late 90s, inflation rates were as low as 2%. The CPI is typically used as a means of adjusting income payments in the future. For example, to maintain purchasing power with a modest 3.0% inflation rate:

$100,000 per year from your investment portfolio at age 45 equals

$180,611 at age 65

$242,726 at age 75

$326,204 at age 85

$378,160 at age 90

However, the CPI is based on the average persons budget. What if your budget is different from the average person? As such, the use of standard or average inflation assumptions is not the most accurate way to project future income needs. The inflation rate should be evaluated each year and adjusted according to your particular income needs in retirement.

An understanding of the purchasing power risk will help you make the most appropriate decisions about the placement of your money in the accumulation stage of your life and the disbursement of your money in the income distribution stage of your life. To apply this concept to your own personal situation, take a look at a completed copy of your Budget Worksheet. When you complete these worksheets, do your best to obtain the most accurate information available. If you use a personal finance computer program, it should be easy to run and print cash flow reports to track your income and expenses. The object is to establish a pretty accurate estimation of your annual income and expenses. With this information at hand, and your projection of future inflation rates, you can calculate your income and expense requirements for many years into the future. It is extremely important to recognize that your income and expense amounts may change over the years. If you were able to go back over the last ten year period and print a cash flow report showing your annual income and expenses, you will surely see different amounts over time. There may be dramatic differences in your annual income and expenses over the years. This is also true during retirement. Spending patterns may vary during retirement depending on whether you are newly retired with plans to pursue an active lifestyle or in your later years with plans to slow down.

The Financial Planning Process

In our firm, we believe in the financial planning process. This is the process of gathering and reviewing financial data, and designing and implementing a plan to help clients reach their goals. It is a lifelong process. Once the plan is in place, it needs to be monitored, reviewed, and updated to meet dynamic circumstances. We believe that everyone can benefit from this process.

So one thing to understand for sure is that your projections will be less accurate for those time periods far into the future. Your income and expense projections for next year will be much more accurate than what you can expect to earn and/or spend ten or twenty years from now. The same is true for projected rates of inflation. You may have to adjust your income and expense projections for the future based on increases or decreases in the inflation rates and for your own personal spending patterns. Here is how an increase of 1% in the inflation rate can affect your purchasing power.

To maintain purchasing power with a 4% inflation rate:

$100,000 per year from your investment portfolio at age 45 equals:

$219,112 at age 65

$324,340 at age 75

$480,102 at age 85

$584,118 at age 90

At age 65, you would need $38,501 per year more with a 4% inflation rate than with a 3% inflation rate. At age 75, you would need almost $81,614 per year more than with a 3% inflation rate. At age 85, you would need over $153,000 per year more than with a 3% inflation rate. These differences are staggering!

What about your spending needs during retirement? Do you anticipate that your expenses will increase or decrease after retirement? Take a look at your average annual expenditures today. You can get this information from your Budget Worksheet. Use the amounts from your most recent Budget Worksheet to complete the following table (see Table 4-1):

T A B L E   4-1

Average Annual Expenditures Today

Item

Food	$_____
Housing	$_____
Apparel and Services	$_____
Transportation	$_____
Health Care	$_____
Entertainment	$_____
Personal Insurance	$_____
Other Expenditures	$_____
Total	$_____

To help you project your spending needs in retirement, we have provided the following table from the U.S. Bureau of Labor Statistics (see Table 4-2):

TABLE 4-2

Average Annual Expenditures By Age Group

ITEM	45 -54	55 -64	65 +
Income before taxes	$122,796	$125,407	$119,223
Income after taxes	115,263	118,063	113,260
Food	9,590	8,838	8,282
Housing	23,592	22,676	20,928
Apparel and Services	3,354	3,387	2,382
Transportation	14,631	14,280	11,857
Health Care	3,628	4,131	6,016
Entertainment	4,273	4,610	3,783
Personal Insurance	12,533	12,435	7,653
Other Expenditures	9,807	9,259	13,984
Total	**$81,407**	**$79,616**	**$74,885**

Source: U.S. Bureau of Labor Statistics; Consumer Expenditures Survey 2003-2004

You will notice that the average annual expenditures decreased in all categories for all age groups with the exception of health care. The average annual expenditures for health care increased by 66% between the 45-54 age group and the 65 and over age group. The Consumer Expenditures Survey 2003-2004 shows a 2.2% reduction in average annual expenditures between the 45-54 age group and the 55-64 age group. It also reveals a 5.9% reduction in expenditures between the 55-64 age group and the 65 and over age group (see Table 4-3).

Although Tables 4-2 and 4-3 reveal an 8.1% decrease in average annual expenditures between the 45-54 age group and the 65 and over age group, the 2003-2004 Consumer Expenditure Survey may not account for long-term health care expenditures. This expenditure would most likely be reflected in a survey of 75 and over age groups if people in nursing homes were able to participate in the survey. If so, average annual health care expenditures would be

TABLE 4-3

	Changes in Average Annual Expenditures By Age	
Age	Average Annual Expenditures	Spending Decreases
45 - 54	$81,407	
55 - 64	$79,616	2.2%
65 +	$74,885	5.9%

Source: U.S. Bureau of Labor Statistics; Consumer Expenditures Survey 2003- 2004

much higher as the need for long-term care increases substantially with age. Keep this factor in mind as you determine how your spending may change during retirement. Incorporating long-term health care expenditures will have a large impact on your total. Insert your own amounts in Table 4-4 based on your own expectation about whether your expenditures will increase or decrease in retirement.

TABLE 4-4

	Estimated Change in Average Annual Expenditures in Retirement	
	Average Annual Expenditures	Spending Increase (Decrease)
Today	$_____	
Retirement	$_____	_____%

Later in the book, we will discuss certain anticipated risks in retirement that will have a dramatic impact on your lifestyle.

After reviewing the information you have provided on the previous worksheets and tables, you will want to attempt to provide a hedge against inflation, especially in the distribution and preservation phase of your life. If you are in the accumulation and protection phase of your life, you will want to attempt to provide a large enough investment portfolio to sustain you for the rest of your life, especially for your core living expenses.

There is no one particular investment portfolio that is appropriate for all individual investors. The optimal portfolio will depend on the amount and timing of cash flow needs, tax considerations and market conditions. Investment decisions should be based therefore, on your objectives. Through that objective driven process, crucial factors such as appropriate levels of risk and return are derived and optimized to achieve those objectives.

Risk and Return Measures

What exactly do we mean by risk and return? Throughout this book, we will ask you about your risk profile, your tolerance for risk and whether the allocation of your portfolio is appropriate for your level of risk. At our firm, we believe in the use of appropriate mathematical measures of risk and return that measure the extent to which returns vary from the average. The primary measurement of the variability of returns is standard deviation. The larger the variability in returns from the average, the greater the standard deviation and the greater the risk. The less variability in returns from the average, the lower the standard deviation and the lower the risk. A standard deviation of 10 means that 68 percent of the time, the returns will fall between plus or minus 10% of the mean. When choosing investments, investors will prefer the least amount of risk for a given expected return. In constructing investment portfolios, the primary measure of risk-adjusted return is the Sharpe Ratio. The Sharpe ratio is derived by dividing the return in excess of the risk free rate by the standard deviation of the investment portfolio. The appropriate measure of risk for a bond's exposure to changes in interest rates is duration. Duration is the weighted average time it takes a bondholder to receive the interest and principal repayments. In general, the higher the duration the more the price of a bond will decline in response to an increase in interest rates.

Efficient Market Hypothesis (EMH)

The Efficient Market Hypothesis is based on the assumption that since investors have equal access to all known information about a security in the capital markets, this information is already reflected in the price of the security. In an efficient market, stock prices adjust instantaneously to the arrival of all new information. According to the Efficient Market Theory:

1) An investor cannot outperform or "beat the market."

2) Stock prices are neither undervalued nor overvalued.

3) The return on an investment is based on the amount of risk an investor is willing to accept.

According to this theory, an investor cannot pick an undervalued security based on the belief that he or she has access to information not publicly available to all investors. In reality, there are questions as to how efficient the financial markets really are and the degree of any exceptions to market efficiency. To address this issue, three forms of the theory have been developed based on the level of information available to investors.

1) **Weak form.** The weak form of the EMH suggests that the use of technical analysis is of no value in trying to find undervalued or overvalued securities. Technical analysis describes the process of using historical information, such as trading volume, historical prices, odd lot transactions and rate-of-return to find undervalued or overvalued securities. However, fundamental analysis can help investors find undervalued or overvalued securities. Fundamental analysis de-

scribes the process of analyzing financial and non-financial information about a company.

2) **Semi-strong form.** The semi-strong form of the EMH suggests that both technical analysis and fundamental analysis are of no value in trying to find undervalued or overvalued securities. Only information that is not publicly available may enable investors to find an undervalued or overvalued security. Note: The use of "inside information" is illegal.

3) **Strong form.** The strong form of the EMH suggests that not even private information will help in finding undervalued or overvalued securities. Since all information, whether public or private, is accessible by all investors, this type of information is already reflected in the stock price.

In our firm, we believe in the weak form of the EMH. We reject the use of technical analysis described above. Since only a small percentage of the variability of a portfolio's return can be attributed to market timing, we also reject the use of market timing.

Growth Versus Value Styles

While it is generally believed that the financial markets are efficient as described above, questions as to the level of efficiency have led to the identification of certain exceptions. One observation is based on the conclusion of the Fama/French research that value equity portfolios provide superior performance over time. Value stocks are those with high book to market value ratios. Growth stocks are those with low ratios of book value to market value. There is no assurance, however, that value equity portfolios will outperform growth portfolios in any particular year. As such, we believe that an appropriate weighting for both value equity portfolios and growth allocations in the broad market is an acceptable approach to balance out these issues.

Active Versus Passive Management

The Efficient Market Hypothesis (EMH) implies that passive management would be the most acceptable approach in a truly efficient market. In fact, various studies of mutual fund performance frequently show the inability of actively managed funds to outperform their indices. Although it is rare to find a manager with a consistent record of out performance, we believe that the choice between active versus passive management is not one of either/or. Since we believe that some markets are more efficient than others, we use both active and passive management (exchange traded funds and index mutual funds). In general, we believe that large cap stocks are very efficient and that small caps, the international arena and real estate markets are less efficient, allowing active managers to take advantage of opportunities in these less efficient markets.

Asset Allocation

The asset allocation decision is determined in response to an investors financial needs and goals. The way assets are allocated or divided among the various asset classes is a significant determinant of long-term portfolio performance. In working with our clients, we help them determine whether a strategic or tactical allocation strategy is appropriate for them. In maintaining a strategic allocation strategy, we take the effects of taxes and transaction costs into consideration. In developing a strategic allocation, we prefer managers who have clearly defined philosophies and who do not drift significantly away from their objective styles. In maintaining a tactical allocation strategy, rebalancing is based on a more opportunistic view of the economic environment.

Portfolio Optimization

In the process of designing an allocation model of asset classes with the highest potential return for a given level of risk, we use a sophisticated optimization program. Since the optimization process is as much an art as it is a science, the weightings and development of input data (estimates about future returns) require the advanced knowledge of an experienced investor or wealth manager. Minor changes in assumptions can have a significant effect on portfolio recommendations due to the optimizer's sensitivity to the input data. Selecting which asset classes to include in a given portfolio depends on each person's risk tolerance level and an awareness of other individual constraints. Limitations should be placed on the percentage that each asset class will represent in the portfolio. The final portfolio recommendations should be based on the constrained optimizers solution for matching an appropriate diversification strategy to the level of risk being managed.

Time Diversification

Just as the goal of diversifying a portfolio among many asset classes is to reduce risk, the risk of increasing equity exposure in a portfolio decreases as the time horizon of the goal increases. As a practical matter, funds required in fewer than five years should be placed in money market mutual funds or fixed income securities with maturity dates equal to or less than the goals time horizon.

Professional Money Management

Over time, professional money managers will generate results far superior to that of any individuals direct security selection and management. This is due to the fact that the management of investment assets is a difficult and time-consuming process requiring advanced knowledge. As such, many individuals prefer to use the services of a fee-only or fee-based financial planner to develop an investment plan for them. Unlike advisors who are compensated through sales commissions, fee-only or fee-based advisors are primarily compensated for constructing financial plans and/or from investment management fees based on a percentage of assets under management. In the latter case, the individual can execute the plan using the entire universe of public and institutional funds offering the best alternatives for the superior management of multiple asset class portfolios. Investment managers should be selected and evaluated based on their philosophies, processes and people. Once selected, a manager may outperform the market in some periods and under perform the market in others. Since frequent switching from one manager to another in an attempt to "beat the market" will in all likelihood fail to achieve higher returns, a manager should be allowed periods of inferior investment performance if he or she remains consistent with his or her philosophy and process. Evaluation of managers should entail a detailed review of all available pertinent information, including both fundamental qualitative and return factor analyses. However, the ultimate decision to hire or fire should be based on fundamental data. Performance measurement should be against appropriate benchmarks, not broad market indices. He or she should be replaced immediately if the portfolio implementation strays significantly from the stated philosophy or process.

On-going Reviews and Management

Initially, individuals must set their own goals in time and dollar specificity. After the portfolio recommendations are implemented by acquiring individual assets, there should be regular reviews of a person's situation to determine if he or she is continuing to move in the direction of achieving his or her goals. This includes revisions in strategic allocations as a result of revised assumptions or changing circumstances or goals. In our practice, we continue to educate our clients, always remaining sensitive to the volatility of each person's individual expectations. We try to make sure that our clients 'stay the course' with a minimum of emotional pain. The focus should always be on the achievement of one's goals, not the performance of the portfolio.

Investing is serious business. After all it is your future. As you can probably understand from reading this brief introduction to investment theory, it can be valuable to have a team of experts backed by a disciplined process on your side. Later in the book, I will show you how you can find some of the industry's most talented professionals to work with you.

In the next chapter, we will discuss the process used to determine the amount of money needed to provide a specific income.

Summary

This chapter was about the critical issues for retirement income planning.

> The first objective for retirement income planning is to make sure that you cannot outlive your money, especially for your core expenses.

> The second objective is to retain your purchasing power by attempting to provide a hedge against inflation, especially in the distribution and preservation phase of your life. If you are in the accumulation and protection phase of your life, you will want to attempt to provide a large enough investment portfolio to sustain you for the rest of your life, especially for your core living expenses.

> Finally, with information abundant and readily available, you could opt to go it alone. It can be very challenging, however, to do the specific financial analysis and investment research needed to secure your financial well being for the long term. In Chapter 10, you will learn how to find a qualified professional to work with you.

Chapter Notes

Chapter 5

Income Planning

"Money isn't everything as long as you have enough."
– Malcolm Forbes

Here comes the fun part! After you have at least three known variables, such as your target rate of return, the number of years in retirement and your retirement income goal, you can determine the amount of money needed to provide you with that income. To get started, complete the appropriate table with the numbers pertaining to your specific needs, circumstances and goals. If you are in the accumulation and protection stage of life (typically between the ages of 35 and 65), you will complete the first (Pre-Retirement) table with your retirement income goal in today's dollars and in the year that you expect to retire. In other words, you will adjust your income goal to reflect the effects of inflation over time. Using Appendix A, find the number of years to retirement presented vertically along the left-hand margin and the expected inflation rate presented horizontally at the top of the table. The corresponding interest factor represents the value in the future of one dollar invested today for various combinations of compounding periods and interest rates. If you are in the income distribution and preservation stage of life, you will complete the second (Retirement) table only.

Pre-Retirement

Accumulation and Protection Stage of Life Cycle

Your current age? _____   Spouse? _____

Your age at retirement? _____   Spouse? _____

Number of years until retirement _____   Spouse? _____

Estimated number of years in retirement? _____ Spouse?_____

Annual retirement income goal (in today's dollars)? _____

Estimated inflation rate? _____ Target rate of return? _____

Annual retirement income goal (at age of retirement)? _____

Retirement

Income Distribution and Preservation Stage of Life Cycle

Your current age? _____   Spouse? _____

Estimated number of years in retirement? _____ Spouse? _____

Annual retirement income goal (in today's dollars)? _____

Estimated inflation rate? _____ Target rate of return? _____

For example, to maintain purchasing power with a modest 4.0% inflation rate:

$100,000 per year from your investment portfolio at age 45 equals

$219,110 at age 65 ($100,000 X 2.1911)

$324,340 at age 75 ($100,000 X 3.2434)

$480,100 at age 85 ($100,000 X 4.8010)

$584,120 at age 90 ($100,000 X 5.8412)

To maintain purchasing power with a 5% inflation rate:

$100,000 per year from your investment portfolio
at age 45 equals:

$265,330 at age 65 ($100,000 X 2.6533)

$432,190 at age 75 ($100,000 X 4.3219)

$704,000 at age 85 ($100,000 X 7.0400)

$898,500 at age 90 ($100,000 X 8.9850)

Of course, you can also solve these calculations with a financial calculator with an internal rate of return function. Or you can use one of use one of the many problem solvers available on the Internet. We have many useful problem solvers available right on our website at wegriffith.com.

Many people depend on a fixed income stream during retirement. However, in an inflationary environment, a fixed income stream will not allow one to maintain a constant standard of living due to rising prices over the years. In the last chapter, we discussed the critical issues in retirement income planning. The second objective we discussed and illustrated in the various tables was how important it is to retain your purchasing power by attempting to provide a hedge against inflation, especially in the distribution and preservation phase of your life. Therefore, a more appropriate means of providing an income stream over the years is to have your retirement income increase annually with inflation.

For example, to receive the equivalent of $150,000 in today's dollars at the beginning of each year increasing at the rate of 3%, each successive payment would be adjusted for inflation as illustrated in the following table (see Table 5-2). The annual income values can be obtained by multiplying the annual income goal by the appropriate future value factor (see Appendix A). Note: When using Appendix A, the annual income for Year 2 is derived by multiplying the annual income goal of $150,000 by the future value factor in Period 1 (1.0300), which is the first compounding period. The annual income for Year 3 is derived by multiplying the annual income goal of $150,000 by the future value factor in Period 2 (1.0609), which is the second compounding period.

TABLE 5-2

Year	Annual Income	Year	Annual Income
1	$150,000	19	255,360
2	154,500	20	263,025
3	159,135	21	270,915
4	163,905	22	279,045
5	168,825	23	287,415
6	173,895	24	296,040
7	179,115	25	304,920
8	184,485	26	314,070
9	190,020	27	323,490
10	195,720	28	333,195
11	201,585	29	343,185
12	207,630	30	353,490
13	213,870	31	364,095
14	220,275	32	375,015
15	226,890	33	386,265
16	233,700	34	397,845
17	240,705	35	409,785
18	247,920		

The amount of money needed to provide a particular income stream over a thirty-five year period depends on the assumed after-tax rate of return on the investments. It is important to understand that in the real world the after-tax rate of return on investments is not the same every year. The actual return on investment portfolios will vary from year to year based on the composition of assets within the portfolio and changing market conditions as illustrated in Table 5-3.

TABLE 5-3

Annual Returns of a 50/50 Portfolio of Stocks/Bonds

Year	Annual Return	Year	Annual Return
1	16.99%	11	1.82%
2	4.00%	12	21.50%
3	12.25%	13	18.64%
4	23.11%	14	10.11%
5	2.93%	15	1.26%
6	1.88%	16	-1.73%
7	7.21%	17	-5.92%
8	9.92%	18	16.39%
9	-0.80%	19	7.65%
10	28.02%	20	3.67%

Average Annual Return 8.95%

*For illustrative purposes only and not indicative of any investment.
This illustration is based on information compiled by the author reflecting
the historical performance of the S&P 500® and the Lehman Brothers
Aggregate Bond indices over a recent 20-year period..*

The following table shows the amounts received at the beginning of each of the next thirty-five years, discounted annually based on an after-tax return of 8% (see Table 5-4). The discounted values can be obtained by multiplying the annual income in each year by the appropriate present value factor (see Appendix B). The amount received in year one is not discounted because the present value of $150,000 received at the beginning of the first year is $150,000. The year two income of $154,500 is multiplied by .9259 to obtain the discounted value of $143,052. In year three, $159,135 is multiplied by .8573 and so on.

TABLE 5-4

Year	Annual Income	Discounted Value	Year	Annual Income	Discounted Value
1	$150,000	$150,000	19	$255,360	$63,891
2	154,500	143,052	20	263,025	60,943
3	159,135	136,426	21	270,915	58,111
4	163,905	130,108	22	279,045	55,446
5	168,825	124,086	23	287,415	52,856
6	173,895	118,353	24	296,040	50,416
7	179,115	112,878	25	304,920	48,086
8	184,485	107,647	26	314,070	45,854
9	190,020	102,668	27	323,490	43,736
10	195,720	97,899	28	333,195	41,716
11	201,585	93,374	29	343,185	39,775
12	207,630	89,053	30	353,490	37,929
13	213,870	84,928	31	364,095	36,191
14	220,275	80,995	32	375,015	34,501
15	226,890	77,256	33	386,265	32,910
16	233,700	73,662	34	397,845	31,390
17	240,705	70,262	35	409,785	29,914
18	247,920	67,013		Total	$2,623,325

You would need an investment portfolio of $2,623,325 to provide an initial payment of $150,000 with each additional annual payment adjusted for inflation until the total portfolio is entirely depleted in the thirty-fifth year.

Now, it is your turn. Complete the following table with the assumptions you are using to achieve your retirement income goal (see Table 5-5).

Step One – Write your annual income goal for the first year of retirement on the first line next to year 1.

Step Two – Complete the table with your annual income goal for year two on by multiplying your first year income goal by the appropriate future value factor based on your expectation of future inflation rates (see Appendix A).

Step Three – Complete the table with the discounted values. The year one discounted value would be the same as the annual income for the first year. In year two, multiply the annual income shown on that line by the present value factor for the appropriate year and target rate of return (see Appendix B). For example, in Table 5-4, the annual income in year five is $168,825. To obtain the discounted value in year five, you simply multiply $168,825 by .7350.

Step Four – Continue this process for the expected number of years in retirement.

Step Five – Add the discounted values for all years. This is the total amount of money needed to provide an inflation-adjusted income for that number of years.

It might be a good time at this point to restate what we said in Chapter 4 regarding the financial planning process. We discussed how financial planning is a lifelong process and that once your plan is in place, it needs to be monitored, reviewed and updated to meet dynamic circumstances. It is crucial to remember that your projections will be less accurate for those time periods well into the future. For the examples in this chapter, we made certain assumptions in the process of arriving at the total investment portfolio needed to provide a series of inflation-adjusted payments. But this was for a time period of thirty-five years. A lot can change over that length of time. Your income and expense projections may change. The same is true for projected rates of inflation. There is no doubt that you will have to adjust your income and expense projections for the future based on increases or decreases in the inflation rates. You will also have to adjust your target rate of return due to changing market conditions. In the real world, the return on investment portfolios is not the same every year – hence the need to monitor, rebalance and update portfolios based on changing circumstances, financial needs and market conditions.

TABLE 5-5

Year	Annual Income (_____X Future Value Factor)	Discounted Value (_____X Present Value Factor)	Year	Annual Income (_____X Future Value Factor)	Discounted Value (_____X Present Value Factor)
1	$_____	$_____	26	$_____	$_____
2	$_____	$_____	27	$_____	$_____
3	$_____	$_____	28	$_____	$_____
4	$_____	$_____	29	$_____	$_____
5	$_____	$_____	30	$_____	$_____
6	$_____	$_____	31	$_____	$_____
7	$_____	$_____	32	$_____	$_____
8	$_____	$_____	33	$_____	$_____
9	$_____	$_____	34	$_____	$_____
10	$_____	$_____	35	$_____	$_____
11	$_____	$_____	36	$_____	$_____
12	$_____	$_____	37	$_____	$_____
13	$_____	$_____	38	$_____	$_____
14	$_____	$_____	39	$_____	$_____
15	$_____	$_____	40	$_____	$_____
16	$_____	$_____	41	$_____	$_____
17	$_____	$_____	42	$_____	$_____
18	$_____	$_____	43	$_____	$_____
19	$_____	$_____	44	$_____	$_____
20	$_____	$_____	45	$_____	$_____
21	$_____	$_____	46	$_____	$_____
22	$_____	$_____	47	$_____	$_____
23	$_____	$_____	48	$_____	$_____
24	$_____	$_____	49	$_____	$_____
25	$_____	$_____	50	$_____	$_____
	Total $_____			**Total** $_____	

Summary

The objective we discussed and illustrated in this chapter was how important it is to retain your purchasing power by attempting to provide a hedge against inflation, especially in the distribution and preservation phase of your life.

In an inflationary environment, a fixed income stream will not allow one to maintain a constant standard of living due to rising prices over the years. A more appropriate means of providing an income stream over the years is to have your retirement income increase annually with inflation.

After you have at least three known variables, such as your target rate of return, the number of years in retirement and your retirement income goal, you can determine the amount of money needed to provide that income using the simple five-step process described in this chapter.

Chapter Notes

Chapter 6

Strategies for a Changing Lifestyle

"There are so many things that we wish we had done yesterday, so few that we feel like doing today." - Mignon McLaughlin

Retirement life in the future will be a time of great excitement for those who finally achieve their dreams and also a time of anxiety as they confront many complex and expensive issues over an extended period of time. How much you need to finance your retirement depends on, among other things, how well you want to live and the expected length of your retirement life. Do you want to maintain an unchanged standard of living in retirement or increase your standard of living to accommodate an extensive travel schedule, start a new business or career, provide financial help to family members or take up the time you are no longer spending at work with a new hobby or activity? In either case, you need to calculate how much you should save through personal investments to finance your retirement life. You can project your annual expenditures in retirement by using the tables and worksheets in Chapter 4. How much you need to accumulate depends on the lifestyle you envision. Do you want to make sure that you never outlive your money, especially for your basic living and health care expenses? Are you saving enough? Where do you stand?

Where Do You Stand?

In our practice, we meet with our clients every three months to deliver a comprehensive Quarterly Performance Review showing exactly where they stand in relation to their goals and objectives.

Before you can develop an investment plan, you first need to know exactly what your financial position is today.

What Are Your Investable Resources?

What is the combined value of all those assets earmarked for retirement? _____

You can get this information from the Retirement Accumulations Worksheet that you completed in Chapter 1.

What is the allocation of your current portfolio (in stocks, bonds and cash)?

<u>Current Portfolio</u>

Cash _____

Stocks

    Domestic

        Large Cap

            Growth _____

            Value _____

        Mid Cap

            Growth _____

            Value _____

Small Cap

    Growth   _____

    Value   _____

Foreign

    Emerging markets   _____

Bonds

    Short term   _____

    Intermediate term _____

    Long term   _____

Real Estate

    REITs   _____

Total Portfolio Value   _____

Based on an analysis of your current investment portfolio, you can determine where you are in terms of risk and return. Does the risk/return profile of your current investment portfolio match your risk tolerance? In our firm, we believe that a client's risk tolerance is a significant constraint in the wealth management process.

Investment Policy

We believe in developing client specific investment strategies that emphasize diversified asset allocation. The Investment Policy Statement outlines the strategy that is just right for each person. It sets the framework for the particular investment portfolio appropriate based on individual needs, objectives and risk tolerance.

What is the allocation of your target portfolio (in stocks, bonds and cash)?

__Target Portfolio__

Cash   _____

Stocks

     Domestic

         Large Cap

            Growth   _____

            Value   _____

         Mid Cap

            Growth   _____

            Value   _____

         Small Cap

            Growth   _____

Value   _____

Foreign

    Emerging markets   _____

Bonds

    Short-term   _____

    Intermediate term   _____

    Long-term   _____

Real Estate

    REITs   _____

Total Portfolio Value   _____

With a diversified asset allocation strategy, you hold more than one asset class in your portfolio in an attempt to reduce risk. This occurs because you will be limiting the effect that any one-asset class will have on the performance of your portfolio. Since stocks and bonds generally do not react to changing market conditions in the same way, declines in the total returns of one asset class may be offset by increases in the returns of other asset classes (see Exhibit 6-1).

    Although it is impossible to reduce risk completely, diversification can reduce the overall volatility of your portfolio. One of the advantages of diversification is that the performance of your portfolio will be less dependent on the return of one asset class. By investing in different asset classes with offsetting returns, you can attempt to protect your portfolio against major losses. A more volatile one-asset class portfolio may achieve a higher return over a longer period of time than a diversified portfolio. The object of diversification, however, is to reduce risk over the long run (see Exhibit 6-2).

E X H I B I T 6-1

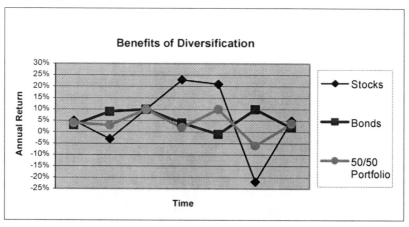

For illustrative purposes only and not indicative of any investment.

E X H I B I T 6-2

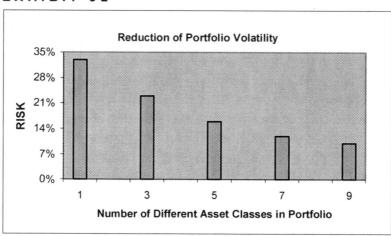

For illustrative purposes only and not indicative of any investment.

Effectively matching your risk/return profile to your target portfolio will provide the optimal portfolio for your particular risk level (see Exhibit 6-3).

EXHIBIT 6-3

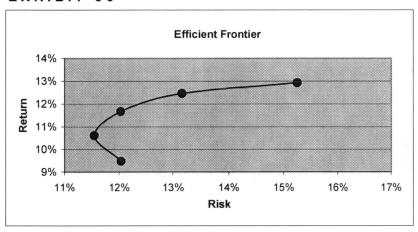

For illustrative purposes only and not indicative of any investment.

The efficient frontier identifies the highest returning portfolio for any level of risk. Likewise, for any level of return the efficient frontier identifies the lowest risk portfolio. The portfolio with the highest return and highest risk is the more volatile one-asset class portfolio. At each point along the efficient frontier, there are portfolios corresponding to a combination a risk/return measures suitable for each individual risk preference. The areas outside of the efficient frontier represent portfolios that are not feasible (above the line) or inefficient (below the line).

Exhibit 6-4 provides a historical illustration of each risk/return profile, reflecting the historical combined performance of specific indices representing the target asset allocation for each of four risk/return profiles for the period 1986-2005.

EXHIBIT 6-4

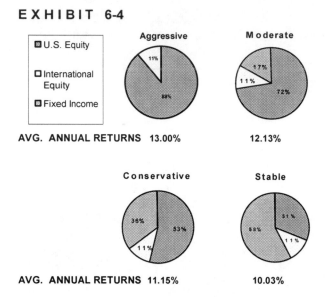

For illustrative purposes only and not indicative of any investment.
Investment returns, past, hypothetical or otherwise are not indicative
of future performance.

You can now begin to develop the investment strategy that is right for you. There are a variety of ways to implement your investment strategy. The universe of public and institutional funds offers an acceptable alternative for the superior management of multiple asset class portfolios. In our firm, we use both actively managed mutual funds and passively managed funds, such as index mutual funds and exchange traded funds. We exercise care in the appropriate place-ment of investments within taxable and tax-deferred accounts.

The Power of Compounding

In the previous section and throughout this book, you will learn about the benefits of diversification and how combining multiple asset classes can reduce the overall risk and volatility of your portfo-lio. The key to enhancing the return from your investment portfolio is by reinvesting the income produced by your investments. This could be income from interest, dividends and/or capital gains. You will adversely affect your ability to achieve your long-term objectives if you consume or spend rather than reinvest your income and gains. If you do not consume or spend your income and gains, the growth of your portfolio will be enhanced by the power of compounding. The effects of compounding over time can be enhanced even further by starting early (see Exhibit 6-5).

E X H I B I T 6-5

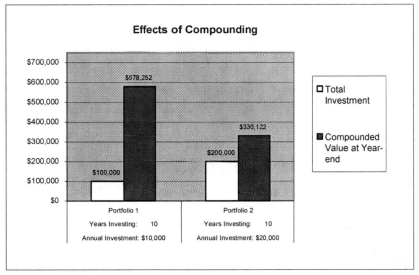

This exhibit provides a hypothetical illustration based on information compiled by the author reflecting the historical performance of the S&P 500®

Portfolio 1 is a hypothetical illustration of an investor who began investing in stocks in 1985, investing $10,000 each year for 10 years through to 1995. For the next 10 years from 1995 to 2005, the portfolio was allowed to grow without any additional contributions. The $100,000 outlay grew to a portfolio value of $578,252. Portfolio 2 is a hypothetical illustration of an investor who began investing in stocks in 1995, investing $20,000 each year for 10 years through to 2005. The $200,000 outlay grew to a portfolio value of $330,122. The ending wealth of Portfolio 1 for the investor who started sooner was an astounding $248,130 more than that of Portfolio 2, even though the total outlay in Portfolio 1 was half that of Portfolio 2. Compounding can increase the likelihood that your investment plan will be successful over the long term.

Monitoring and Rebalancing

Once your plan is in place, it needs to be monitored, reviewed and updated to meet dynamic circumstances. Your personal circumstances as well as market conditions and the economic environment change over time. As time passes, different asset classes grow at different rates. Because of these changes, your investment portfolio will need to be rebalanced to the strategic or tactical asset allocation.

Here's a look at how the two asset allocation approaches differ and how a target asset mix may need to be rebalanced over time:

Strategic Asset Allocation

Target Asset Mix	Change Over Time	Rebalanced Portfolio
Stocks ____70%____	Stocks ____85%____	Stocks ____70%____
Bonds ____20%____	Bonds ____15%____	Bonds ____20%____
Cash ____10%____	Cash ____0%____	Cash ____10%____

The initial target mix of the portfolio is 70% stocks, 20% bonds and 10% cash. As time passes, stocks outperform both cash and bonds. The target mix of the portfolio has changed over time and is rebalanced to the strategic allocation.

Tactical Asset Allocation

Target Asset Mix	Stocks are Undervalued	Stocks are Overvalued
Stocks ___70%___	Stocks ___90%___	Stocks ___50%___
Bonds ___20%___	Bonds ___10%___	Bonds ___40%___
Cash ____10%___	Cash _____0%___	Cash ____10%___

The initial target mix of this portfolio is also initially 70% stocks, 20% bonds and 10% cash. With a tactical asset allocation strategy, adjustments can be made to your portfolio at any time to capitalize on changes in the capital market. If for example, you believe that stocks are undervalued, a full 90% may be invested in stocks. If you believe that the stock market is overvalued, the exposure may be reduced to 50%.

The Dangers of Market Timing

In our firm, we believe that attempting to time the market is not a sound investment strategy. In Chapter 4, we mentioned that only a small percentage of the variability of a portfolio's return could be attributed to market timing. Furthermore, successful market timing on a consistent, regular basis is extremely difficult. It may even have a negative effect on portfolio performance since investors who attempt to time the market run the risk of missing those periods of exceptional rates of return for each asset class. Exhibit 6-6 illustrates how a hypothetical investment of $500,000 invested in the S&P 500® at the end of 1985 grew to $4,743,610. That same investment of $500,000 would have grown to only $1,516,094 if it missed the five best years of returns for the S&P 500®.

EXHIBIT 6-6

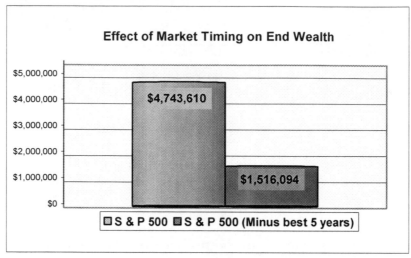

This exhibit provides a hypothetical illustration based on information compiled by the author reflecting the historical performance of the S&P 500®

Can You Stay The Course?

In our firm, we believe that there should be regular reviews of a client's situation to determine if he or she is continuing to move in the direction of achieving his or her goals. Our responsibility is to assure that our clients 'stay the course' with a minimum of emotional pain. We believe that a client's risk tolerance is a significant constraint in the wealth management process. It is easy to follow a long-term strategy during good times when your portfolio is receiving positive returns, but what if your portfolio declines in the midst of a bear market to less than its original value?

What Would You Do?

❑ Develop a more aggressive strategy in an attempt to recover your losses.

❑ Maintain your present disciplined, long-term strategy.

❑   Move your investments to a more conservative portfolio to avoid losing any more money.

If you were holding a well-diversified portfolio, the answer would be to 'stay the course' (see Exhibit 6-7).

E X H I B I T   6-7

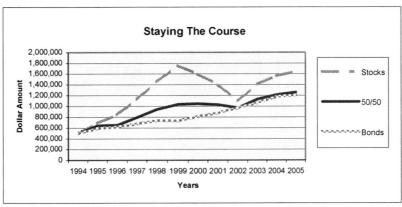

This exhibit provides a hypothetical illustration based on information compiled by the author reflecting the historical performance of the S&P 500® and the Lehman Brothers Aggregate Bond indices.

At the beginning of this chapter, we said that the process of building financial security requires a commitment to managing your investments in a way that enables you to achieve your goal. If you want to achieve your goal of financial independence and freedom for tomorrow, you must be committed to managing and coordinating your financial decisions today. If you want to make sure that you never outlive your money, especially for your basic living and health expenses and maintain your financial freedom and independence, then you must continually monitor your investment portfolio and adjust your portfolio to meet dynamic circumstances.

     When making long-term investment decisions for your retirement portfolio, you should compare the returns of different asset classes both before and after inflation (see Exhibit 6-8).

E X H I B I T 6-8

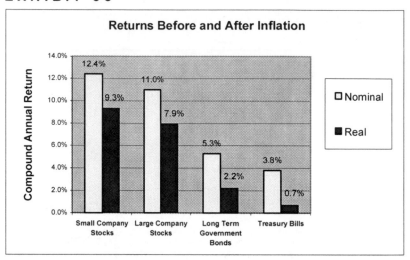

This exhibit provides a hypothetical illustration based on information compiled by the author reflecting the historical performance of specific indices.

Note that after adjusting for inflation, treasury bills barely kept pace with rising prices over the years. Since inflation will erode your purchasing power over time, the objective illustrated in previous chapters is to retain your purchasing power by attempting to provide a hedge against inflation, especially in the distribution and preservation phase of your life. Therefore, an acceptable means of providing an income stream over the years is to have your retirement income increase annually with inflation. In constructing your investment portfolio, return requirements should be based on real rates of return. This is the inflation-adjusted return. This differs from the rate of return you typically think of when discussing the return on investments. These unadjusted returns are referred to as the nominal returns. An overly conservative portfolio with large allocations to cash and bonds may not provide you with a real rate of return sufficient enough to keep pace with rising prices in your retirement years.

To re-emphasize the point about how a fixed income stream will not allow a retiree to maintain a constant standard of living, the following examples will compare the difference between one portfolio that provides an income stream that increases annually with inflation and another portfolio that provides a fixed income stream.

Inflation-Adjusted Portfolio 1

Assume you want to receive the equivalent of $200,000 in today's dollars at the beginning of each year for the next thirty years (your estimated number of years in retirement). In order to retain your purchasing power, you want your retirement income from your investment portfolio to increase annually with inflation. Additionally, you expect that inflation will average 3% and your assumed target rate of return on your investments will be 8% after taxes. To receive the equivalent of $200,000 in today's dollars at the beginning of each year, each successive payment would be adjusted annually for inflation as illustrated in Table 6-1.

TABLE 6-1

Year	Annual Income ($200,000 X Future Value Factor)	Year	Annual Income ($200,000 X Future Value Factor)
1	$200,000	16	$311,600
2	206,000	17	320,940
3	212,180	18	330,560
4	218,540	19	340,480
5	225,100	20	350,700
6	231,860	21	361,220
7	238,820	22	372,060
8	245,480	23	383,220
9	253,360	24	394,720
10	260,960	25	406,560
11	268,780	26	418,760
12	276,840	27	431,320
13	285,160	28	444,260
14	293,700	29	457,580
15	302,520	30	471,320

You can now determine the amount of money needed to provide you with enough retirement income to last for the entire thirty-year period. Each of the income payments in the previous table must be discounted to reflect your ability to earn the assumed after-tax return of 8%. The following table shows the amounts received at the beginning of each of the next thirty years, discounted annually for the after-tax return on your investment portfolio (see Table 6-2).

TABLE 6-2

Year	Annual Income	Discounted Values (Annual Income X Present Value Factors)	Year	Annual Income	Discounted Values (Annual Income X Present Value Factors)
1	$200,000	$200,000	16	$311,600	$98,216
2	206,000	190,735	17	320,940	93,682
3	212,180	181,902	18	330,560	89,350
4	218,540	173,477	19	340,480	85,188
5	225,100	165,449	20	350,700	81,257
6	231,860	157,804	21	361,220	77,482
7	238,820	150,504	22	372,060	73,928
8	245,480	143,529	23	383,220	70,474
9	253,360	136,890	24	394,720	67,221
10	260,960	130,532	25	406,560	64,115
11	268,780	124,499	26	418,760	61,139
12	276,840	118,737	27	431,320	58,314
13	285,160	113,237	28	444,260	55,621
14	293,700	107,993	29	457,580	53,034
15	302,520	103,008	30	471,320	50,573
				Total	$3,277,890

You would need an investment portfolio of $3,277,890 to provide an initial payment of $200,000 with each additional annual payment adjusted for inflation until the total portfolio is completely consumed in the thirtieth year.

Unadjusted Portfolio 2

Assume you want to receive the equivalent of $200,000 at the beginning of each year for the next thirty years (your estimated number of years in retirement). In this portfolio, however, your retirement income will remain the same each year for thirty years. Your assumed target rate of return on your investments will be 8% after taxes. To receive the fixed-income payments in the amount of $200,000 at the beginning of each year, each successive payment would remain the same as illustrated in Table 6-3.

TABLE 6-3

Year	Annual Income	Year	Annual Income
1	$200,000	16	$200,000
2	200,000	17	200,000
3	200,000	18	200,000
4	200,000	19	200,000
5	200,000	20	200,000
6	200,000	21	200,000
7	200,000	22	200,000
8	200,000	23	200,000
9	200,000	24	200,000
10	200,000	25	200,000
11	200,000	26	200,000
12	200,000	27	200,000
13	200,000	28	200,000
14	200,000	29	200,000
15	200,000	30	200,000

Now you can determine the amount of money needed to ensure that you will have enough retirement income to last for the entire thirty-year period. Each of the income payments in the previous table must be discounted to reflect your ability to earn the assumed after-tax return of 8%. The following table shows the amounts received at the beginning of each of the next thirty years discounted annually for the after-tax return on your investment portfolio (see Table 6-4).

TABLE 6-4

Year	Annual Income	Discounted Value (Annual Income X Present Value Factors)	Year	Annual Income	Discounted Value (Annual Income X Present Value Factors)
1	$200,000	$200,000	16	$200,000	$63,040
2	200,000	185,180	17	200,000	58,380
3	200,000	171,460	18	200,000	54,060
4	200,000	158,760	19	200,000	50,040
5	200,000	147,000	20	200,000	46,340
6	200,000	136,120	21	200,000	42,900
7	200,000	126,040	22	200,000	39,740
8	200,000	116,700	23	200,000	36,780
9	200,000	108,060	24	200,000	34,060
10	200,000	100,040	25	200,000	31,540
11	200,000	92,640	26	200,000	29,200
12	200,000	85,780	27	200,000	27,040
13	200,000	79,420	28	200,000	25,040
14	200,000	73,540	29	200,000	23,180
15	200,000	68,100	30	200,000	21,460
				Total	**$2,431,640**

You would need an investment portfolio of $2,431,640 to provide annual payments of $200,000 until the total portfolio is entirely dissipated in the thirtieth year. The first thing you should notice is that with the inflation-adjusted portfolio, the total amount needed at the beginning of the retirement period is $846,250 more than the beginning value of the unadjusted portfolio. This is a significant difference in the beginning values of the two portfolios. However, the inflation-adjusted portfolio will enable you to retain your purchasing power and your standard of living as your retirement income from your investment portfolio will increase annually with inflation.

What if inflation is substantially higher than 3% as in the following example?

Assume you want to receive the equivalent of $200,000 in today's dollars at the beginning of each year for the next thirty years (your estimated number of years in retirement). In order to retain your purchasing power, you want your retirement income from your investment portfolio to increase annually with inflation. Additionally, you expect that inflation will average 5% and your assumed target rate of return on your investments will be 8% after taxes. To receive the equivalent of $200,000 in today's dollars at the beginning of each year, each successive payment would be adjusted annually for inflation as illustrated in Table 6-5.

TABLE 6-5

Year	Annual Income ($200,000 X Future Value Factor)	Year	Annual Income ($200,000 X Future Value Factor)
1	$200,000	16	$415,780
2	210,000	17	436,580
3	220,500	18	458,400
4	231,521	19	481,320
5	243,100	20	505,400
6	255,260	21	530,660
7	268,020	22	557,200
8	281,420	23	585,060
9	295,500	24	614,300
10	310,260	25	645,020
11	325,780	26	677,280
12	342,060	27	711,140
13	359,180	28	746,700
14	377,120	29	784,020
15	395,980	30	823,220

Now you can determine the amount of money needed to provide you with that income and dissipate the total amount entirely at the beginning of the thirtieth year. Each of the income payments in the previous table must be discounted to reflect your ability to earn the assumed after-tax return of 8%. The following table shows the assumed after-tax return of 8%. The following table shows the amounts received at the beginning of each of the next thirty-five years, discounted annually for the after-tax return on your investment portfolio (see Table 6-6).

TABLE 6-6

Year	Annual Income ($200,000 X Future Value Factor)	Discounted Value (Annual Income X Present Value Factors)	Year	Annual Income ($200,000 X Future Value Factor)	Discounted Value (Annual Income X Present Value Factors)
1	$200,000	$200,000	16	$415,780	$131,054
2	210,000	194,439	17	436,580	127,438
3	220,500	189,035	18	458,400	123,906
4	231,521	183,781	19	481,320	120,426
5	243,100	178,679	20	505,400	117,101
6	255,260	173,730	21	530,660	113,827
7	268,020	168,906	22	557,200	110,716
8	281,420	164,209	23	585,060	107,593
9	295,500	159,659	24	614,300	104,615
10	310,260	155,192	25	645,020	101,720
11	325,780	150,901	26	677,280	98,883
12	342,060	146,710	27	711,140	96,146
13	359,180	142,630	28	746,700	93,487
14	377,120	138,667	29	784,020	90,868
15	395,980	134,831	30	823,220	88,332
				Total	$4,107,481

You would need an investment portfolio of $4,107,481 to provide an initial payment of $200,000 with each additional annual payment adjusted for inflation until the total portfolio is completely depleted in the thirtieth year. The first thing you should notice is that the total amount needed at the beginning of the retirement period is $829,591 more than the beginning value of the 3% inflation-adjusted portfolio. If inflation were to continue at the higher rate of 5%, your retirement lifestyle could be effected dramatically as the cost of basic living and healthcare expenses become much more expensive. The important thing to remember about both scenarios is that an inflation-adjusted portfolio will enable you to retain your purchasing power and your standard of living as your retirement income from your investment portfolio will increase annually with inflation.

Are You There Yet?

Now you should compare the amount of money needed to that of your current investable resources. How do the two figures compare?

What is the combined value of all those assets earmarked for retirement? _____

What is the total lump sum of money needed to provide you with $ _____ at the beginning of each year for _____ years?

If both amounts are close, fantastic! You may be on track and moving in the direction of achieving your retirement income goal. If the value of your current portfolio is less, then you should review your situation to determine how much more you need to accumulate to reach your retirement goal. This may include revisions in strategic allocations as a result of revised assumptions or changing circumstances or goals. Is your asset allocation aligned with your risk/return profile? The plan you devise for your particular situation will depend on whether you are in the accumulation and protection stage or the income distribution and preservation stage. Are you still working? How long do you expect to continue working? If you still have plenty of time until you retire, you should determine how much more you need to accumulate to reach your retirement goal.

Assuming you are still working, how long do you expect to continue working? _____

If you expect to continue working, you can determine how much more you will need to save through personal investments to accumulate the difference between what you have now and what you will need. Assume you want to receive the equivalent of $250,000 in today's dollars at the beginning of retirement and each year thereafter for thirty years (your estimated number of years in retirement). In order to retain your purchasing power, you want your retirement income from your investment portfolio to increase annually with inflation. Additionally, you expect that inflation will average 3% and your assumed target rate of return on your investments will be 7% after-taxes. To receive the equivalent of $250,000 in today's dollars at the beginning of each year, each successive payment would be adjusted annually for inflation as illustrated in Table 6-7.

TABLE 6-7

Year	Annual Income ($250,000 X Future Value Factor)	Year	Annual Income ($250,000 X Future Value Factor)
1	$250,000	16	$389,500
2	257,500	17	401,180
3	265,225	18	413,200
4	273,175	19	425,600
5	281,375	20	438,380
6	289,825	21	451,530
7	298,525	22	465,080
8	307,475	23	479,030
9	316,700	24	493,400
10	326,200	25	508,200
11	335,980	26	523,450
12	346,050	27	539,150
13	356,450	28	555,330
14	367,125	29	571,980
15	378,150	30	589,150

You can now determine the amount of money needed to provide you with enough retirement income to last for the entire thirty-year period. Each of the income payments in the previous table must be discounted to reflect your ability to earn the assumed after-tax return of 7%. The following table shows the amounts received at the beginning of each of the next thirty years, discounted annually for the after-tax return on your investment portfolio (see Table 6-8).

TABLE 6-8

Year	Annual Income	Discounted Values (Annual Income X Present Value Factors)	Year	Annual Income	Discounted Values (Annual Income X Present Value Factors)
1	$250,000	$250,000	16	$389,500	$141,155
2	257,500	240,660	17	401,180	135,880
3	265,225	231,648	18	413,200	130,819
4	273,175	222,993	19	425,600	125,935
5	281,375	214,661	20	438,380	121,212
6	289,825	206,645	21	451,530	116,675
7	298,525	198,907	22	465,080	112,317
8	307,475	191,495	23	479,030	108,117
9	316,700	184,319	24	493,400	104,058
10	326,200	177,420	25	508,200	100,166
11	335,980	170,779	26	523,450	96,419
12	346,050	164,408	27	539,150	92,842
13	356,450	158,264	28	555,330	89,353
14	367,125	152,357	29	571,980	86,026
15	378,150	146,647	30	589,150	82,834
				Total	$4,555,011

You would need an investment portfolio of $4,555,011 to provide an initial payment of $250,000 with each additional annual payment adjusted for inflation until the total portfolio is completely consumed in the thirtieth year. Now assume that you are 35 years of age, the value of your current portfolio earmarked for retirement is $225,000 and you plan to retire at the age of 67. You can now determine how much you will need to save through personal investments to accumulate the difference between what you have now and what you will need. You will need an investment portfolio of approximately $4,555,011.

The value of your current retirement portfolio is projected to increase to $1,960,936 in 32 years.

You will need to accumulate an additional $2,594,171 within 32 years.

In this case, you will need to invest $23,537 at the end of each year for 32 years.

$2,594,171 divided by 110.2182 (see Appendix C for the appropriate divisor).

Now, it's your turn. Complete the following paragraphs and tables with the assumptions you are using to achieve your retirement income goal.

If you are still working, how long do you expect to continue working?

_____

If you expect to continue working, you can determine how much you will need to save through personal investments to accumulate the difference between what you have now and what you need.

I want to receive the equivalent of $ _____ in today's dollars at the beginning of each year for _____ years (my estimated number of years in retirement). In order to retain my purchasing power, I want my retirement income from my investment portfolio to increase annually with inflation. I expect that inflation will average _____ % and my assumed target rate of return on my investments will be _____ % after taxes. To receive the equivalent of $ _____ in today's dollars at the beginning of each year, each successive payment would be adjusted annually for inflation as illustrated in Table 6-9.

TABLE 6-9

Year	Annual Income ($____X Future Value Factor)	Year	Annual Income ($____X Future Value Factor)
1	$_____	26	$_____
2	$_____	27	$_____
3	$_____	28	$_____
4	$_____	29	$_____
5	$_____	30	$_____
6	$_____	31	$_____
7	$_____	32	$_____
8	$_____	33	$_____
9	$_____	34	$_____
10	$_____	35	$_____
11	$_____	36	$_____
12	$_____	37	$_____
13	$_____	38	$_____
14	$_____	39	$_____
15	$_____	40	$_____
16	$_____	41	$_____
17	$_____	42	$_____
18	$_____	43	$_____
19	$_____	44	$_____
20	$_____	45	$_____
21	$_____	46	$_____
22	$_____	47	$_____
23	$_____	48	$_____
24	$_____	49	$_____
25	$_____	50	$_____

Now you can determine the amount of money needed to provide you with that income and dissipate the total amount entirely at the beginning of the _____ year. Each of the income payments in the previous table must be discounted to reflect your ability to earn the assumed after-tax return of _____%. The following table shows the amounts received at the beginning of each of the next _____ years, discounted annually for the after-tax return on your investment portfolio (see Table 6-10).

TABLE 6-10

Year	Annual Income (X Future Value Factor)	Discounted Value (X Present Value Factor)	Year	Annual Income (X Future Value Factor)	Discounted Value (X Present Value Factor)
1	$_____	$_____	26	$_____	$_____
2	$_____	$_____	27	$_____	$_____
3	$_____	$_____	28	$_____	$_____
4	$_____	$_____	29	$_____	$_____
5	$_____	$_____	30	$_____	$_____
6	$_____	$_____	31	$_____	$_____
7	$_____	$_____	32	$_____	$_____
8	$_____	$_____	33	$_____	$_____
9	$_____	$_____	34	$_____	$_____
10	$_____	$_____	35	$_____	$_____
11	$_____	$_____	36	$_____	$_____
12	$_____	$_____	37	$_____	$_____
13	$_____	$_____	38	$_____	$_____
14	$_____	$_____	39	$_____	$_____
15	$_____	$_____	40	$_____	$_____
16	$_____	$_____	41	$_____	$_____
17	$_____	$_____	42	$_____	$_____
18	$_____	$_____	43	$_____	$_____
19	$_____	$_____	44	$_____	$_____
20	$_____	$_____	45	$_____	$_____
21	$_____	$_____	46	$_____	$_____
22	$_____	$_____	47	$_____	$_____
23	$_____	$_____	48	$_____	$_____
24	$_____	$_____	49	$_____	$_____
25	$_____	$_____	50	$_____	$_____
		Total $_____			Total $_____

I would need an investment portfolio of $_____ to provide an initial payment of $_____ with each additional annual payment adjusted for inflation until the total portfolio is entirely dissipated in the _____ year. I am _____ years of age, the value of my current portfolio earmarked for retirement is $_____ and I plan to retire at the age of _____. I can now determine how much I will need to save through personal investments to accumulate the difference between what I have now and what I will need.

I will need an investment portfolio of approximately $_____.

The value of my current retirement portfolio is projected to increase to $_____ in _____ years.

I will need to accumulate an additional $_____ within _____ years.

In this case, I will need to invest $_____ at the end of each year for _____ years.

$_____ (additional accumulation) divided by_____ (see Appendix C for the appropriate divisor).

Unfortunately, many people put off planning for retirement until just before retirement. A study by the U.S. Department of Health and Human Services found that only 1 percent of the population retired wealthy, 4 percent were financially secure, 20 percent had to continue to work and 49 percent were dependent on Social Security as their primary source of income. Are you close to retirement or already in the income distribution and preservation stage of your life? If the value of your current portfolio is less than the amount needed to provide you with your retirement income goal, then you should review your situation to determine what steps you can take from here. You may have several options. You may be able to find new sources of income, delay retirement, reduce your living expenses, try to increase your investment return, or use a combination of these options. The plan you devise for your particular situation will depend on your goals, your current financial situation, including your net worth, your current and projected expenses, and your sources of income.

Assume that you are close to retirement and you expect to continue working for 17 more years. You can now determine how much you will need to save through personal investments to accumulate the difference between what you have now and what you need.

For example, say you want to receive the equivalent of $450,000 in today's dollars at the beginning of each year for the next thirty years (your estimated number of years in retirement). In order to retain your purchasing power, you want your retirement income from your investment portfolio to increase annually with inflation. Additionally, you expect that inflation will average 3% and your assumed target rate of return on your investments will be 7% after-taxes. To receive the equivalent of $450,000 in today's dollars at the beginning of each year, each successive payment would be adjusted annually for inflation as illustrated in Table 6-11.

TABLE 6-11

Year	Annual Income ($450,000 X Future Value Factor)	Year	Annual Income ($450,000 X Future Value Factor)
1	$450,000	16	$701,100
2	463,500	17	722,115
3	477,405	18	743,760
4	491,715	19	766,080
5	506,475	20	789,075
6	521,685	21	812,745
7	537,345	22	837,135
8	553,455	23	862,245
9	570,060	24	888,120
10	587,160	25	914,760
11	604,755	26	942,210
12	622,890	27	970,470
13	641,610	28	999,585
14	660,825	29	1,029,555
15	680,670	30	1,060,470

You can now determine the amount of money needed to provide you with enough retirement income to last for the entire thirty-year period. Each of the income payments in the previous table must be discounted to reflect your ability to earn the assumed after-tax return of 7%. The following table shows the amounts received at the beginning of each of the next thirty years, discounted annually for the after-tax return on your investment portfolio (Table 6-12).

TABLE 6-12

Year	Annual Income	Discounted Values (Annual Income X Present Value Factors)	Year	Annual Income	Discounted Values (Annual Income X Present Value Factors)
1	$450,000	$450,000	16	$701,100	$254,079
2	463,500	433,187	17	722,115	244,580
3	477,405	416,966	18	743,760	235,474
4	491,715	401,387	19	766,080	226,683
5	506,475	386,390	20	789,075	218,179
6	521,685	371,961	21	812,745	210,013
7	537,345	358,033	22	837,135	202,168
8	553,455	344,692	23	862,245	194,609
9	570,060	331,775	24	888,120	187,305
10	587,160	319,356	25	914,760	180,299
11	604,755	307,397	26	942,210	173,555
12	622,890	295,935	27	970,470	167,115
13	641,610	284,875	28	999,585	160,833
14	660,825	274,242	29	1,029,555	154,845
15	680,670	263,964	30	1,060,470	149,102
				Total	$8,198,999

You would need an investment portfolio of $8,198,999 to provide an initial payment of $450,000 with each additional annual payment adjusted for inflation until the total portfolio is entirely depleted in the thirtieth year. Now assume that you are 50 years of age, the value of your current portfolio earmarked for retirement is $2,000,000 and you plan to retire at the age of 67. You can now determine how much you will need to save through personal investments to accumulate the difference between what you have now and what you will need.

You will need an investment portfolio of approximately $8,199,199.

The value of your current retirement portfolio is projected to increase to $6,317,630 in 17 years.

You will need to accumulate an additional $1,881,563 within 17 years.

In this case, you will need to invest $61,010 at the end of each year for 17 years.

$1,881,563 divided by 30.8402 (see Appendix F).

In Chapter 2, we showed how in at least two of the four different households, the couples were at risk of outliving their money. This is despite the fact that they had existing portfolios and they were continuing to save for the future. One solution would be for each couple to save more. Studies show that although most people are aware that they should be saving more for retirement, many are not doing so. In the two scenarios illustrated in Chapter 2, both couples were already saving as much as they possibly could. What can be done to increase accumulations if projections show that many retirees will come up short of the income needed to finance their retirement?

Do you know how much more you should be saving for retirement and how you will do it?

Equity Management

Households own more than $14 trillion in real estate assets.[2] This is almost twice the amount they hold in mutual funds and stocks. In two of the hypothetical scenarios in Chapter 2, each couple owned a home worth $350,000. Suppose they could reduce their current monthly mortgage payments and redirect their savings toward their retirement goal. Typically, homeowners who want to manage payment risk opt for fixed-rate mortgages. Fixed-rate mortgages allow homeowners to payoff their loan when interest rates fall. When interest rates fall, homeowners can lower their mortgage payments by refinancing and even extract some of the built-up equity in the process. But if interest rates rise, there is no increase in monthly payments with a fixed-rate mortgage loan. However, there is no free lunch. Homeowners pay for the right to refinance and for the insurance against increasing mortgage payments in the form of higher fixed rates. During a February 2004 Governmental Affairs Conference in Washington, D.C., Federal Reserve Chairman Alan Greenspan said that "calculations by market analysts of the "option adjusted spread" on mortgages suggest that the cost of these benefits conferred by fixed-rate mortgages can range from 0.5 percent to 1.2 percent, raising homeowners' annual after-tax mortgage payments by several thousand dollars." Recent research within the Federal Reserve suggests that many homeowners would have saved tens of thousands of dollars over the last decade if they had adjustable-rate mortgages instead of fixed-rate mortgages.[3] By opting for a lower interest adjustable-rate mortgage or even a low rate interest-only ARM, the two couples in our hypothetical scenarios could redirect the difference between their current monthly mortgage payment and a new lower payment towards retirement savings in a tax-favorable environment. Since the primary objective is to increase the funds available to invest for retirement, this option works best for people who are not concerned with reducing the loan balance on their home. This strategy is most appropriate for sophisticated borrowers who understand that most of the equity build-up in their homes can be attributed to appreciation and not principal reduction. These borrowers also know that paying down the principal on their loans results in "dead equity." Here is how this option can free up money for investing. Suppose that our homeowners in scenario one (the DeWalts) have a $280,000 mortgage loan on their personal residence with a fair market value (FMV) of $350,000. Assume that their current mortgage payment is $2,054.54 or $24,654 per year (based on an 8% 30-year conventional fixed-rate loan). If they can refinance with a 5% interest-only ARM (initial fixed-rate for first ten years), their new payment would be $1,166.67 per month or $14,000 per year (see Table 6-13).

TABLE 6-13

Year	8% 30-Yr. Loan	5% ARM	Savings
1	$24,654	$14,000	$10,654
2	24,654	14,000	10,654
3	24,654	14,000	10,654
4	24,654	14,000	10,654
5	24,654	14,000	10,654
6	24,654	14,000	10,654
7	24,654	14,000	10,654
8	24,654	14,000	10,654
9	24,654	14,000	10,654
10	24,654	14,000	10,654
Total	$246,540	$140,000	$106,540

With the interest-only ARM, they are able to free up $106,540 over a ten-year period for investing. Assuming they could invest their savings at an 8% rate of return, they could end up with $166,688 after ten years (see Table 6-14). What happens after ten years? They could refinance back into a low interest-only ARM to keep their mortgage payments low. You can see how the balance would continue to grow over the years by investing the savings in a tax-deferred annuity. The previous illustration is based on the assumption that our homeowners had an existing $280,000 mortgage loan. What if they owned their home debt free? They would essentially have $350,000 in "dead equity" tied up in their personal residence. Assume they could refinance and take out $315,000 of equity to invest for retirement. Once again, if they refinance with a 5% interest-only ARM, their payment would be $15,750 per year (see Table 6-15).

T A B L E 6-14

Year	8% Tax-Deferred Annuity
1	$11,506
2	23,933
3	37,354
4	51,849
5	67,503
6	84,410
7	102,669
8	122,389
9	143,686
10	166,688

T A B L E 6-15

Year	5% ARM Loan	After-Tax Cost
1	$15,750	$14,350
2	15,750	14,350
3	15,750	14,350
4	15,750	14,350
5	15,750	14,350
6	15,750	14,350
7	15,750	14,350
8	15,750	14,350
9	15,750	14,350
10	15,750	14,350
Total	$157,500	$143,500

If they transfer the $315,000 to a fixed-index annuity with an 8% return, they could end up with $680,060 after a period of only ten years (see Table 6-16). The balance would continue to grow until retirement, after which they could start receiving payments.

T A B L E 6-16

Year	Beginning Balance	8% Growth	Ending Balance
1	$315,000	$25,200	$340,200
2	340,200	27,216	367,416
3	367,416	29,393	396,809
4	396,809	31,745	428,554
5	428,554	34,284	462,838
6	462,838	37,027	499,865
7	499,865	39,989	539,854
8	539,854	43,188	583,042
9	583,042	46,643	629,685
10	629,685	50,375	680,060

Fixed-index annuities are ideal for those who want to participate in market returns without the market risk. In essence, a fixed-index annuity provides a guaranteed income stream over time like its fixed-interest annuity counterpart. But unlike the fixed return with a fixed annuity, a fixed-index annuity provides for increased growth in returns linked to an equity-index, such as the S&P 500® Index. A recent study by The Advantage Compendium, Ltd., a research firm in St. Louis, Missouri, found that over a five-year period – from January 2, 1997 to January 2, 2002, the average combined annualized return of fixed-index annuities was 8.3 percent, outperforming CDs and bond funds (5.6 percent annually).[4] In addition, the study found that fixed-index annuities outperformed 61 percent of all mutual funds during that same time period. Since fixed-index annuities provide principal protection in down markets, they are ideal vehicles to use in combination with the equity financing strategy described above. In Chapter 3, we introduced three risks that people face in retirement; the market risk, the risk of not saving enough and the longevity risk. In this chapter, we provide an innovative and dynamic financial solution for managing both the risk of not saving enough and the market risk. First, by lowering current mortgage payments, the difference can be invested to create more wealth for retirement.

Second, by transferring funds to a fixed-index annuity, retirement accumulations can be protected from market risk. Note: This is an innovative program that is not typically available through any bank or mortgage broker. Like any financial planning technique, you should objectively review the proposition of converting equity in your home to borrowed money for use in other investments. With an interest-only ARM, you need to understand which index the ARM uses, how and when rates are adjusted, the margin, yearly and lifetime caps and the potential for negative amortization. Additionally, you should seek the objective advice of a qualified practitioner for information about the advantages and disadvantages of various mortgage loan programs and for information about the variety of fixed-index annuities.

This chapter started with a brief introduction to investment theory after which we went through the process for computing the amount of money needed to provide a retirement income for an expected number of years. We ended this chapter by providing an innovative and dynamic financial solution for managing both the risk of not saving enough and the market risk. In the next chapter, we will discuss the income distribution process in light of increased longevity, and how to manage this risk with a combination of methods to assure that retirement portfolios last for life rather than for some predetermined period of time.

Summary

One of the main factors you need to consider when investing is the amount of risk you are willing to accept to obtain a particular return on your investments. Over the long term, periods of high returns tend to offset periods of low returns resulting in a dispersion of returns gravitating towards the average. Additionally, the range of returns is less volatile over longer holding periods.

The main point to understand about the concept of diversification is that by maintaining a well-diversified portfolio, you are attempting to manage the risk of your portfolio over the long term, allowing you to maintain a disciplined, long-term strategy.

Based on your retirement objectives, you can determine how much money you will need to provide an inflation-adjusted income each year over your expected retirement lifetime and the additional money, if any, you will need to save through personal investments to accumulate the difference between what you have now and what you will need.

References

[1] U.S. Department of Health and Human Services.
[2] 2004 Governmental Affairs Conference, Federal Reserve Chairman Alan Greenspan.
[3] 2004 Governmental Affairs Conference, Federal Reserve Chairman Alan Greenspan.
[4] The Advantage Compendium, Ltd.

Chapter 7

Income Distribution: Making Your Retirement Income Last for Life

"An economist is an expert who will know tomorrow why the
things he predicted yesterday didn't happen today."
– Laurence J. Peter

In Chapter 3, we introduced three risks that people face in
retirement. All three have one thing in common – uncertainty.
The goal of this chapter is to address the longevity risk and the
market risk. Each can have profound implications for those nearing
or in retirement. Market risk refers to the possibility that your
portfolio will lose value due to changes in conditions in the capital
markets. Longevity risk refers to the fact that longer life expectancies
increase the risk of outliving your money in retirement.

How long do you want your retirement income to last? Ten,
twenty, thirty years? What are the chances that you will live to be
100 years of age or older? If you worry about outliving your money,
you may under-spend during retirement thus having a sub-optimal
retirement. If you overspend during retirement, you may simply run
out of money.

Since the future is unknown, successful planning today
requires more complex, innovative and dynamic financial solutions
to provide a retirement income and to protect against the risk of
increasing long-term financial obligations. In this chapter, we will
explore the issue of portfolio liquidation using a combination of
methods to manage longevity and the market risk.

How Long Will Your Money Last?

During the retirement years, the challenge is to assure that one will never outlive their money, especially for basic living and healthcare expenses. This is our mission when planning for our client's future. The sustainability of your investment portfolio will depend to a great extent on the rate at which you liquidate your portfolio to provide your annual retirement income. In previous chapters, we discussed the enemy of retirement – inflation – and how an inflation-adjusted income is the most acceptable means of providing a retirement income to retain one's standard of living. The amount of this income as a percentage of your entire investment portfolio is considered to be the withdrawal rate. Based on the information derived in Chapter 6, an investment portfolio of $3,277,890 should provide an initial payment of $200,000 with each additional annual payment adjusted for inflation until the total portfolio is completely consumed in the thirtieth year. The following table illustrates the withdrawal rate over the thirty-year period. (See Table 7-1)

The income projections and corresponding withdrawal rates were derived from the following data:

Life expectancy after retirement _____30 years_____

Target portfolio rate of return _____8%_____

Inflation rate _____ 3%_____

Annual inflation-adjusted income __$200,000_____

Unfortunately, you do not know for certain exactly how long you will live, the future rate of inflation and your target portfolio's future investment returns. The best you can do, it seems, is to make predictions about your own mortality and the future. It should be obvious from the previous illustration that a change in the annual in-

TABLE 7-1

Year	Inflation-Adjusted Income ($200,000 X X FV Factor)	Portfolio Value (Beginning of Period)	Withdrawal Rate
1	$200,000	$3,277,890	6.10%
2	206,000	3,324,121	6.20%
3	212,180	3,367,571	6.30%
4	218,540	3,407,822	6.40%
5	225,100	3,444,425	6.50%
6	231,860	3,476,870	6.60%
7	238,820	3,504,611	6.80%
8	245,980	3,527,054	7.00%
9	253,360	3,543,560	7.10%
10	260,960	3,553,416	7.30%
11	268,780	3,555,852	7.60%
12	276,840	3,550,038	7.80%
13	285,160	3,535,054	8.10%
14	293,700	3,509,885	8.40%
15	302,520	3,473,480	8.70%
16	311,600	3,424,637	9.10%
17	320,940	3,362,080	9.50%
18	330,560	3,284,431	10.10%
19	340,480	3,190,181	10.70%
20	350,700	3,077,677	11.40%
21	361,220	2,945,135	12.30%
22	372,060	2,790,628	13.30%
23	383,220	2,612,053	14.70%
24	394,720	2,407,140	16.50%
25	406,560	2,173,413	18.80%
26	418,760	1,908,202	22.10%
27	431,320	1,608,597	27.10%
28	444,260	1,271,459	35.40%
29	457,580	893,375	52.30%
30	471,320	470,658	100%

come, inflation rate, rate of return and/or life expectancy would either increase or decrease the withdrawal rate. For example, an increase in the annual inflation adjusted income from $200,000 per year to $250,000 per year would increase the withdrawal rate as

TABLE 7-2

Year	Inflation-Adjusted Income ($250,000 X FV Factor)	Portfolio Value (Beginning of Period)	Withdrawal Rate
1	$250,000	$3,277,890	7.60%
2	257,500	3,270,121	7.90%
3	265,225	3,253,631	8.20%
4	273,175	3,227,478	8.50%
5	281,375	3,190,647	8.80%
6	289,825	3,142,014	9.20%
7	298,525	3,080,364	9.70%
8	307,475	3,004,386	10.20%
9	316,700	2,912,664	10.90%
10	326,200	2,803,641	11.60%
11	335,975	2,675,636	12.60%
12	346,050	2,456,644	13.70%
13	356,450	2,279,442	15.10%
14	367,125	2,076,831	17.00%
15	378,150	1,846,482	19.50%
16	389,500	1,585,799	23.20%
17	401,175	1,292,003	28.80%
18	413,200	962,094	38.50%
19	425,600	592,805	59.70%
20	438,375	180,582	100.00%

shown in Table 7-2. An increase in the annual inflation adjusted income from $200,000 per year to $250,000 per year would increase the withdrawal rate substantially, thus dissipating the entire portfolio in 20 years or ten years sooner than expected!

The object of income distribution planning is to increase the likelihood of sustaining your investment portfolio for the rest of your life. This will depend to a great extent on your ability to stabilize the rate at which you liquidate your portfolio to provide your annual retirement income. This book is all about planning a retirement income for the rest of your life. Since you do not know for certain exactly how long you will live, how do you handle the uncertainty regarding the length of your life in retirement? In previous chapters, we provided illustrations based on predictions about the future rate of inflation, your target portfolios future investment returns and your estimated length of life in retirement. The illustrations show the rate at which you can liquidate your portfolio to provide an annual inflation-adjusted income until the total portfolio is entirely depleted in a specified year. This outcome would be acceptable if you are exactly right about the ultimate length of your life in retirement. But if your predictions are wrong, you may outlive the 'planned for' period and run out of money. If you run out of money, you may end up living on Social Security benefits and a company pension plan (if you have one). We cannot overstress the importance of addressing the issue of uncertainty regarding the length of your life in retirement.

Longevity Management

One way to manage the longevity risk is by converting a portion of your investment portfolio into a **commercial** annuity that will provide a stream of income guaranteed to last for the rest of your life. In much the same way that multiple asset classes with different rates of return can be combined in a portfolio in order to reduce the market risk, the addition of an annuity to a portfolio can be used to hedge the longevity risk. Throughout this book, we have been illustrating how the systematic liquidation of capital can provide an income to last for a specified period of time. This can also be considered an annuity. But the type of annuities referred to here are commercial annuities developed by insurance companies to guarantee an income for the rest of one's life, no matter how long that is. These annuities provide protection against living too long.

There is considerable variation in the types of annuities available and the annuity interest rates, even among competitive annuity providers. The challenge is to select the most appropriate type of annuity for your particular portfolio after assessing your retirement income needs. In other words, based on the asset allocation of your investment portfolio, which asset classes can effectively be converted into an annuity? In general, fixed annuities most resemble the cash and fixed income portion of a well-diversified portfolio. As such, an annuity may represent an alternative to the cash and bond allocations of your portfolio, but unlike cash and bonds, annuities can provide a guaranteed income for the rest of your life. In the process of converting a portion of your portfolio into an annuity, you should refer to the worksheets pertaining to the accumulation of your retirement nest egg. This is where you derive the amount of money needed to provide an inflation-adjusted income stream. Based on your particular risk/return profile, you should know the allocation of the asset classes in your target portfolio. What percentage of the asset mix applies to cash and bonds? Can you convert a portion of your portfolio to an annuity and still receive essentially the same inflation-adjusted income for the length of your retirement life? For example, consider the following hypothetical example of a $3,277,890 investment portfolio (see Exhibit 7-1).

E X H I B I T   7-1

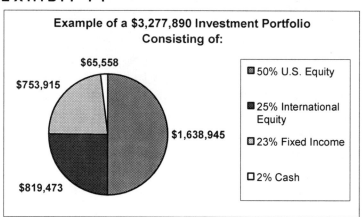

For illustrative purposes only and not indicative of any investment.

In this hypothetical example, there is $819,473 allocated to cash and fixed income investments. By comparing the various annuity options available, you can derive the income payments one could receive at various ages. The following table illustrates the difference (for males and females) in the amount of monthly income payments at various ages (see Table 7-3).

TABLE 7-3

Monthly Income For Each $1,000		
	Life Annuity	
Age	Male	Female
65	8.91	7.96
66	9.15	8.16
67	9.42	8.40
68	9.71	8.60
69	10.02	8.89
70	10.35	9.22
For illustrative purposes only		

A 67-year old male could receive $90,432 per year by converting $800,000 from the cash and fixed income positions to an immediate annuity. In the previous example, we show that you would need an investment portfolio of $3,277,890 to provide an initial payment of $200,000 with each additional annual payment adjusted for inflation until the total portfolio is entirely dissipated in the thirtieth year. By converting $800,000 to an immediate annuity, the value of the portfolio has been reduced to $2,477,890. After deducting the $90,432 in annual annuity payments, you still need to receive an additional $109,568 in the first year of retirement. Since the annuity payment would provide the same fixed income of $90,432 for life, the difference of $2,477,890 could be invested to provide annual inflation-adjusted payments of $109568.

How would the conversion of a portion of your investment portfolio into a *commercial* annuity effect the rest of your portfolio?

Does the presence of an annuity increase the likelihood that your portfolio will last as long as you do?

In order to retain your purchasing power, you want your retirement income from your investment portfolio to increase annually with inflation. As in the previous illustration, assume that inflation will average 3% and the target rate of return on your investments will be 8% after taxes (see Table 7-4).

TABLE 7-4

Year	Inflation-Adjusted Income ($200,000 X FV Factor) minus $90,432)	Portfolio Value (Beginning of Period)
1	$109,568	$2,477,890
2	115,568	2,557,788
3	121,748	2,637,597
4	128,108	2,717,117
5	134,668	2,796,130
6	141,428	2,874,379
7	148,388	2,951,587
8	155,548	3,027,455
9	162,928	3,101,659
10	170,528	3,173,830
11	178,348	3,243,566
12	186,408	3,310,435
13	194,728	3,373,949
14	203,268	3,433,559
15	212,088	3,488,714
16	221,168	3,538,756
17	230,508	3,582,995
18	240,128	3,620,686
19	250,048	3,651,003
20	260,268	3,673,031
21	270,788	3,685,784
22	281,628	3,688,196
23	292,788	3,679,093
24	304,288	3,657,210
25	316,128	3,621,156
26	328,328	3,569,430
27	340,888	3,500,390
28	353,828	3,412,262
29	367,148	3,303,109
30	380,888	3,155,998

Note: For ease of illustration, we use the same 8% rate of return for this scenario. It is important to understand, however, that by converting $800,000 from the cash and fixed income allocations to an immediate annuity, the remaining allocation to U.S. equity would increase from 50% to approximately 67%. Likewise, the international equity allocation would increase from 25% to approximately 33%. This would, in all likelihood increase the return of the investment portfolio. An increase in the target return for the portfolio is not necessarily a detriment. By converting a portion of the portfolio to an annuity, one may be willing to accept a more aggressive portfolio in return for the guaranteed income stream provided by the commercial annuity. After 30 years of receiving an inflation-adjusted income, you would still have an investment portfolio over $3 million! It is interesting to note how the presence of a commercial annuity reduces the withdrawal rate increasing the lifespan of the investment portfolio.

Here is another hypothetical example of a $3,277,890 investment portfolio (see Exhibit 7-2).

E X H I B I T 7-2

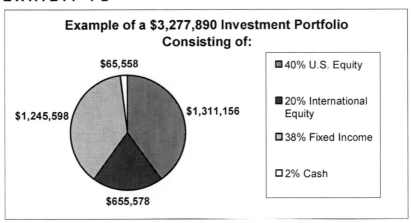

For illustrative purposes only and not indicative of any investment.

In this hypothetical example, there is $1,311,156 allocated to cash and fixed income investments. By comparing the various annuity options available, you can derive the income payments one could receive at various ages. The following table illustrates the difference (for males and females) in the amount of monthly income payments at various ages (see Table 7-5).

TABLE 7-5

Monthly Income For Each $1,000		
	Life Annuity	
Age	Male	Female
65	8.91	7.96
66	9.15	8.16
67	9.42	8.40
68	9.71	8.60
69	10.02	8.89
70	10.35	9.22
For illustrative purposes only		

Based on the following table, a 67-year old male could receive $146,952 per year by converting $1,300,000 from the cash and fixed income positions to an immediate annuity. In the previous example, we show that you would need an investment portfolio of $3,277,890 to provide an initial payment of $200,000 with each additional annual payment adjusted for inflation until the total portfolio is entirely depleted in the thirtieth year. By converting $1,300,000 to an immediate annuity, the value of the portfolio has been reduced to $1,977,890. After deducting the $146,952 in annual annuity payments, you still need to receive an additional $53,048 in the first year of retirement. Since the annuity payment would provide the same fixed income of $146,952 for life, the difference of $1,994,201 could be invested to provide annual inflation-adjusted payments.

How would the conversion of a portion of your investment portfolio into a *commercial* annuity effect the rest of your portfolio?

Does the presence of an annuity increase the likelihood that your

118

portfolio will last as long as you do?

In order to retain your purchasing power, you want your retirement income from your investment portfolio to increase annually with inflation. Once again, assume that inflation will average 3% and the target rate of return on your investments will be 8% after taxes (see Table 7-6).

TABLE 7-6

Year	Inflation-Adjusted Income ($200,000 X FV Factor Minus $146,952)	Portfolio Value (End of Period)
1	$53,048	$1,977,890
2	59,048	2,078,829
3	65,228	2,181,363
4	71,588	2,285,426
5	78,148	2,390,945
6	84,908	2,497,821
7	91,868	2,605,946
8	99,028	2,715,204
9	106,408	2,825,470
10	114,008	2,936,587
11	121,828	3,048,385
12	129,888	3,160,682
13	138,208	3,273,257
14	146,748	3,385,853
15	155,568	3,498,234
16	164,648	3,610,079
17	173,988	3,721,065
18	183,608	3,830,843
19	193,528	3,939,014
20	203,748	4,045,125
21	214,268	4,148,687
22	225,108	4,249,173
23	236,268	4,345,990
24	247,768	4,438,500
25	259,608	4,525,990
26	271,808	4,607,693
27	284,368	4,682,756
28	297,308	4,750,259
29	310,628	4,809,187
30	324,368	4,858,443

Note: For ease of illustration, we use the same 8% rate of return for this scenario. It is important to understand, however, that by converting $1,300,000 from the cash and fixed income allocations to an immediate annuity, the remaining allocation to U.S. equity would increase from 40% to approximately 66%. Likewise, the international equity allocation would increase from 20% to approximately 33%. This would, in all likelihood increase the return of the investment portfolio. An increase in the target return for the portfolio is not necessarily a detriment. By converting a portion of the portfolio to an annuity, one may be willing to accept a more aggressive portfolio in return for the guaranteed income stream provided by the commercial annuity. After 30 years of receiving an inflation-adjusted income, you would still have an investment portfolio of over $4 million! These illustrations show how the presence of an immediate annuity will lengthen the liquidation period of the remaining investment portfolio by reducing the withdrawal rate.

Managing the Market Risk

The possibility that your portfolio will lose value due to changes in market conditions is much more of a risk for most people than the longevity risk. This uncertainty is compounded by the fact that you cannot predict when the next occurrence of an extended market decline or "bear market" will be. An extended market decline soon after retirement could jeopardize the sustainability of withdrawals over the life of the retirement period. Referring back to the beginning of this chapter, we provide an illustration showing that, based on a 3% average inflation rate and rate of return of 8% after taxes, each successive payment would be adjusted annually for inflation as illustrated in Table 7-7.

TABLE 7-7

Year	Annual Income ($200,000 X Future Value Factor)	Year	Annual Income ($200,000 X Future Value Factor)
1	$200,000	16	311,600
2	206,000	17	320,940
3	212,180	18	330,560
4	218,540	19	340,480
5	225,100	20	350,700
6	231,860	21	361,220
7	238,820	22	372,060
8	245,980	23	383,220
9	253,360	24	394,720
10	260,960	25	406,560
11	268,780	26	418,760
12	276,840	27	431,320
13	285,160	28	444,260
14	293,700	29	457,580
15	302,520	30	471,320

You can now determine the amount of money needed to ensure that you will have enough retirement income to last for the thirty-year period. Each of the income payments in the previous table must be discounted to reflect your ability to earn the assumed after-tax return of 8%. The following table shows the amounts received at the beginning of each of the next thirty years, discounted annually for the after-tax return on your investment portfolio (see Table 7-8). You would need an investment portfolio of $3,277,890 to provide an initial payment of $200,000 with each additional annual payment adjusted for inflation until the total portfolio is completely consumed in the thirtieth year (see Table 7-8).

TABLE 7-8

Year	Annual Income ($200,000 X Future Value Factor)	Discounted Value (Annual Income X Present Value Factor)
1	$200,000	$200,000
2	206,000	190,735
3	212,180	181,902
4	218,540	173,477
5	225,100	165,449
6	231,860	157,804
7	238,820	150,504
8	245,980	143,529
9	253,360	136,890
10	260,960	130,532
11	268,780	124,499
12	276,840	118,737
13	285,160	113,237
14	293,700	107,993
15	302,520	103,008
16	311,600	98,216
17	320,940	93,682
18	330,560	89,350
19	340,480	85,188
20	350,700	81,257
21	361,220	77,482
22	372,060	73,928
23	383,220	70,474
24	394,720	67,221
25	406,560	64,115
26	418,760	61,139
27	431,320	58,314
28	444,260	55,621
29	457,580	53,034
30	471,320	50,573
	Total	$3,277,890

What if there is an extended market decline or "bear market" in the first year of retirement? Instead of the portfolio increasing at an average 8% rate of return, assume that the portfolio value declines by 12% per year for the first three years. An extended market decline soon after retirement could jeopardize the sustainability of withdrawals over the life of the retirement period (see Table 7-9).

TABLE 7-9

Year	Annual Income ($200,000 X Future	Portfolio Value (Beginning of Period)	Withdrawal Rate
1	$200,000	$3,277,890	6.1%
2	206,000	2,708,543	7.6%
3	212,180	2,202,238	9.6%
4	218,540	1,751,251	12.4%
5	225,100	1,655,328	13.5%
6	231,860	1,544,646	15.0%
7	238,820	1,417,809	16.8%
8	245,980	1,273,308	19.3%
9	253,360	1,109,514	22.8%
10	260,960	924,646	28.2%
11	268,780	716,781	37.4%
12	276,840	483,841	57.2%
13	285,160	223,562	100 %
14	293,700	0	

After only 13 years of receiving an inflation-adjusted income, the portfolio would be gone! The consequences of having three down years occurring at the beginning of the distribution period can be disastrous. How long do you think it would take to recover from this kind of loss? It might surprise you to know that if the portfolio declines by 32% in a three-year period before distributions begin, it would take six years at an average annual return of 19.64% to catch up to the 8% portfolio (see Table 7-10) – an unrealistic prospect. After distributions begin, however, it is highly unlikely that the portfolio would ever recover even at a much higher rate of return.

TABLE 7-10

Year	Portfolio Value (8% rate of return)	Portfolio Value (negative 12% return years 1,2,3 19.64% next six years)
1	$1,639,761	$1,639,761
2	1,770,942	1,442,990
3	1,912,617	1,269,831
4	2,065,627	1,117,451
5	2,230,877	1,336,918
6	2,409,347	1,599,489
7	2,602,095	1,913,629
8	2,810,262	2,289,466
9	3,035,083	2,739,117
10	3,277,890	3,277,080

How can you manage the market risk without sacrificing the return? In Chapter 6, we showed how fixed-index annuities are ideal for those who want to participate in market returns without the market risk. A fixed-index annuity provides 100% principal protection. Combining a fixed-index annuity with a diversified asset allocation strategy is a unique way to protect a large portion of assets from market declines. A fixed-index annuity could be used in combination with a diversified asset allocation strategy to provide for increased growth in returns linked to an equity-index, such as the S&P 500® Index. In those years with negative market returns, the amount shifted to a fixed-index annuity would not lose money. The account value would remain unchanged. In those years with a positive return, the account value would increase (subject to a "cap" on the increased growth). An ancillary benefit of shifting assets into an annuity is asset protection. This is an especially attractive benefit for those with exposure to liability risks due to their profession or to the types of assets they own. Most all states protect insurance contracts from creditors. Since annuities are insurance contracts, many states also provide some level of creditor protection for these contracts as well. As the protection may vary from state to state, you should always know the specific protections afforded in your state.

Summary

Longevity and a declining market increase the probability that retirement portfolios will be extinguished prematurely. You must continually monitor events, markets and trends and implement innovative and dynamic financial strategies for taking retirement income distributions. In this chapter, we used a combination of methods to manage the market risk and the longevity risk.

While the portfolios containing no annuities were entirely depleted after 30 years of receiving an inflation-adjusted income, the hypothetical retirement portfolios combined with fixed-index annuities were still making payments. Even after 40 or 50 years, the annuities would still be making payments. But what if the hypothetical retiree in our example only lives a short time after retirement? Would he or she lose the balance of the money converted to an annuity? It depends on the payout option selected. Fortunately, there are ways to handle this type of uncertainty. Once again, there is considerable variation in the types of annuities available, the annuity interest rates and the payout options. The challenge is to select the most appropriate type of annuity for your particular portfolio after assessing your retirement income needs.

As you can see, annuities may be a useful tool to help sustain your retirement portfolio in light of the uncertainty regarding the length of your life in retirement and to protect a large portion of assets from market declines increasing the lifespan of the investment portfolios.

Chapter Notes

<u>Longevity Management</u> (P.113)
  - <u>Immediate Fixed Commercial Annuity</u>

Target = 50% of portfolio.
Provides guaranteed income, & Reduces withdrawal Rate.
Get spouse survivor payout option.

<u>Market Risk Management</u> (P.120)
  - <u>Fixed Index Annuity (EX, S&P 500)</u>

Divert portion of Asset Allocation to the Annuity.
Provides protection in market downturns.
Get spouse survivor payout option.

Chapter 8

Addressing Healthcare Risks

"Living longer may not be an issue after all, the high cost of health care could kill you." - Author

I n the last chapter, we introduced the fact that longer life expectancies bring many new challenges to the retirement planning process – namely increased longevity. By the year 2050, over one million Americans are projected to be 100 years of age or older.[1] The goal of this chapter is to address the risk of living longer – with chronic conditions or illnesses that require health care or assistance. Of those who reach the age of 65, 40% will spend time in a nursing home.[2]

During the retirement years, the challenge is to assure that one will never outlive their money, especially for basic living and healthcare expenses. But home health care and nursing home care can be very expensive. The average annual cost of a nursing home stay now exceeds $70,080 per year or $192 per day.[3] The highest rates were reported in the state of Alaska where the cost is $204,765 per year or $561 per day on average. The lowest rates were found in Shreveport, Louisiana were the cost is $36,135 per year or $99 per day. The average length of stay in a nursing home is 2.4 years. Based on these statistics, the average cost of a nursing home stay is approximately $168,192.

This issue can have profound implications in the future. The risk of an unanticipated illness requiring long-term care can rapidly accelerate the liquidation of your assets.

In this chapter, we will explore the issue of health care risks and how to protect your assets from unanticipated long-term care. Every family must consider ways to protect their assets from unanticipated long-term care since:

- Average life expectancies are increasing. Due to advances in medical technology, the number of Americans over the age of 65 is growing rapidly

- The costs for health care are increasing at a rapid rate

- Changing lifestyles make caring for family members exceedingly difficult

- Government programs do not cover the cost for long-term care

Are you prepared for an unanticipated illness or chronic condition that could require long-term health care? For most people, having traditional health insurance that provides coverage for an acute injury or illness is a necessity of life. This type of health insurance coverage is designed to protect against a sudden or acute accident or illness requiring short-term medical attention. But what if your medical and/or functional ability changes to the point where you need assistance with normal everyday activities, such as preparing your meals, shopping, managing your money, using the telephone and cleaning your house. What if you become incompetent or incapacitated and need help with activities of daily living, such as bathing, dressing, toileting, continence, transferring and eating. These are the types of medical conditions that are typically not covered by traditional health insurance programs.

There are many ways to plan a successful retirement while including provisions for long-term care. The risks are high that at some point we will all need long-term care services. Though many people are covered for acute injury or illness with traditional health insurance, many people are financially unprepared for the economic cost of long-term care. If you haven't done so already, it is imperative that you consider ways to protect your assets from the high cost of long-term care.

Long-Term Care Insurance

Long-term care is one of the most overlooked areas of retirement planning. Part of the process of planning for retirement should include an estimation of future long-term care expenses and how to 'protect' your assets against this probability. The longer one lives, the greater the probability of developing conditions requiring long-term care. Although the risk is high, not everyone will incur long-term care expenses. Of those needing long-term care services, some will be able to pay for the services out-of-pocket. Others will spend down their assets sufficiently enough to qualify for Medicaid. For those with large investment portfolios, the idea of self-impoverishment to qualify for medical assistance is not an attractive option. Long-term care insurance is a tool to protect your assets by providing coverage for a broad range of services from home health care to assisted living facilities to nursing home facilities. These services might be needed if you become incompetent or incapacitated and need help with activities of daily living, such as bathing, dressing, toileting, continence, transferring and eating. These are the types of medical conditions that are typically not covered by traditional health insurance programs. Since long-term care costs can consume a significant portion of one's assets, long-term care insurance is becoming an increasingly popular device for funding long-term care expenses. Long-term care insurance will allow you to:

- Protect your retirement portfolio and other assets from depletion.

- Maintain your standard of living.

- Maintain your independence.

- Be able to afford the services needed.

- Avoid dependence on family or government programs.

- Leave an estate to your family.

As the American population ages and medical advances extend life spans, long-term care will become more and more important as a major medical related expense. If you periodically update your balance sheet over the years, you should determine whether, given your financial situation, you should purchase long-term care insurance. One of the most common objections people have to purchasing long-term care insurance is related to the cost. There is a perception that long-term care insurance is too expensive. As you will see in this chapter, the alternative to long-term care insurance, namely self-funding, can really be the most expensive option. This perception is most likely due to a lack of information and understanding about this relatively new form of insurance coverage. Compared to other types of insurance, such as life and health and property and casualty, long-term care insurance is a relatively new form of coverage. Human nature being what it is, most people really do not want to address the issue of needing long-term care services, especially at younger ages. At younger ages, most people are in good health and the issue of needing health care services at some distant time in the future is simply not a priority. Unfortunately, a lack of interest in the matter means that many people will not seek out the necessary information from a qualified source to overcome their misperceptions about the coverage. Many people discover that the cost of the insurance is not really as much as they thought.

In previous chapters, we discussed spending needs in retirement. The success of your retirement plan, may in fact, be based entirely on the accuracy of your estimates. The addition of one unanticipated illness requiring long-term care can have a tremendous impact on your retirement income and the sustainability of your investment portfolio. A thorough analysis of your financial situation will help you decide whether or not you need to purchase the insurance. The following checklist will help you determine how prepared you are for long-term care needs:

1) Review your balance sheet and make a list of all financial assets, such as retirement plans, IRAs, personal investments in stocks, mutual funds, bonds and cash or cash equivalents. You may also include life insurance policies if you can access cash values and/or face values (may require a special long-term care rider).

2) Next, are any of these assets earmarked for specific goals, such as college education funding, retirement, etc.?

3) Determine whether any of your assets could be used to pay for long-term care expenses. You should be sure that these assets or insurance policies are truly discretionary. Otherwise, a need for these funds may preclude you from achieving other goals.

4) You should consider your family situation to determine whether or not your spouse and/or children could provide in home assistance if you were to need care.

This information should help you determine how well you are protected against the financial consequences of long-term care. You may establish that you have sufficient funds to pay for any future long-term care services out of pocket. But do you want to? Many individuals have sufficient funds to pay for losses caused by catastrophic events, but they may not want to. In a way, it is similar to 'protecting' your home and other valuables from the risk of a fire. You may have sufficient funds to rebuild your home, but would you want to? Whenever you consider the impact a major expense will have on your financial well being, insurance is a very cost effective means of protecting yourself and your assets if there is a reasonable chance that you will not experience the expense. If the expense were an absolute certainty, the cost of insurance protection would most likely equal the cost of the expense, in which case your only option would be to pay for the expense yourself.

Premiums for a policy can vary considerably according to age, benefit level, period of coverage and waiting period before coverage begins. The cost of long-term care services can also vary considerably throughout the country.

- Nationally, long-term care costs average more than $42,000 per year. In some parts of the country, the annual cost of long-term care is over $84,000.

- The average stay in a nursing home is roughly 2.3 years with ten percent of those in nursing homes for five or more years.

- The average cost is estimated to be $80,000 per year by 2010.

Source: United Seniors Health Cooperative

The following table is for illustrative purposes only and shows the cost of coverage for a hypothetical person (see Table 8-1).

TABLE 8-1

| Waiting Period: 90 days | | Daily Benefit Amount: $200 | |
| Inflation Rider: 5% | | Benefit Period: Lifetime | |
Age	Annual Premium	Dollar Increase	Percent Increase
47	$2,783		0%
57	$3,385	$602	22%
67	$6,105	$2,720	80%
77	$14,070	$7,965	130%

As you can see from Table 8-1, the cost for coverage goes up substantially with age. This is due, in part, to the higher prevalence of limitations in physical and mental functioning as we age. Even the healthiest people know that their health can change very quickly, even from day to day. A recent study conducted by the American Association for Long-Term Care Insurance (AALTCI) found that the percentage of long-term care insurance applicants who qualify for good health discounts drops for those in their 60s and even more significantly for those in their 70s (see Table 8-2).

TABLE 8-2

Percentage of Applicants Who Qualify for a Good Health Discount			
Age of Applicant	Low	High	Average
40 to 49	50.0%	72.0%	53.7%
50 to 59	42.0%	58.0%	44.2%
60 to 69	27.0%	44.0%	31.9%
70 to 79	15.7%	32.0%	18.8%
80 and over	5.0%	14.0%	11.2%

Source: American Association for Long-Term Care Insurance study of 2005 policy applicants. Data released February 2006.

The potential risk of needing long-term care at some point in the future is high. The previous illustrations highlight the need to investigate options at younger ages while still in good health. A change in health conditions may increase the cost of long-term care insurance substantially. Worse yet, some health conditions can make it difficult, if not impossible, to obtain coverage at any price. It is important to understand, however, that insurers vary in the health conditions that they accept. An applicant may be declined by one insurer but accepted by another.

If you determine that, given your financial situation, you should purchase long-term care insurance, the next step is to review the coverage for policies offered by solid insurance companies (those rated highest by A.M. Best, Standard & Poors and Duff & Phelps). The financial strength of these companies is important since the benefits from these policies may not be needed for many years or decades into the future. Since the cost for coverage in a nursing home can vary, depending on geographic location, you should consider the daily benefit amount appropriate for your planned area of residence after retirement. The cost could vary dramatically from less that $100 per day in one area to over $200 per day in another. In addition, you should know what would trigger the commencement of benefit payments. In most cases, benefits would begin if you were unable to perform two or more activities of daily living, such as bathing, dressing, toileting, continence, transferring and eating. How long would you have to wait before coverage begins? This is called the waiting or elimination period. This is the time period that you would have to pay for long-term care expenses out-of-pocket before the insurance company begins making payments. The cost of the insurance coverage will be lower if you are willing to wait longer before benefits begin. The same is true for the daily benefit amount - the higher the daily benefit, the higher the premium. Two other important factors to consider are the length of the benefit period and whether the policy offers a cost of living adjustment (COLA) rider. Policies typically offer a range of benefit periods, from one year to lifetime.

Although the average stay in a nursing home today is two to three years, you can imagine the implications of having a policy with a limited benefit period. A financial plan based on averages can be dangerous to you wealth. The following illustration is a hypothetical example of those who experience a stay in a nursing home (see Table 8-3). Five people in this illustration were in a nursing home for more than 3 years. It could be financially and emotionally devastating for one to require continued long-term care after the insurance benefits end.

T A B L E 8-3

Insured	Number of Years in Nursing Home
1	5
2	2
3	4
4	2
5	4
6	1
7	5
8	4
9	2
10	1
Average	**3 Years**

Since the length of time one may spend in a nursing home is totally unpredictable, you should consider lifetime coverage if the cost of this coverage is affordable. Although the average annual cost for nursing home care varies throughout the country, the inflation rider available on most policies is for up to a 5% increase in the daily benefit per year. It is highly recommended to add this rider onto your policy for the reasons described above.

The longer we live as a nation, the greater the probability of developing conditions that require long-term care. Without long-term care insurance, individuals risk the total or partial depletion of their asset base.

Self-Insuring

Another way to prepare for the high cost of long-term care is by saving the money needed to cover the out-of-pocket costs of long-term health care. Accumulating a nest egg equal to the total benefits of long-term care insurance policy would require significant planning. Starting to save after retirement is way too late. The following example illustrates the planning process to self-fund potential expenses over a 20-year period. Assume that the average annual cost

($70,080) of a nursing home stay will increase each year at the rate of 5% (see Table 8-4). In 20 years, the average annual cost of care in a nursing home could be as high as $185,900 per year or over $500 per day.

TABLE 8-4

Year	Annual Income ($70,080 X Future Value Factor)
1	$70,080
2	73,584
3	77,263
4	81,125
5	89,443
6	93,914
7	98,610
8	103,543
9	108,715
10	114,153
11	119,858
12	125,857
13	132,143
14	138,751
15	145,689
16	152,978
17	160,623
18	168,655
19	177,082
20	185,943

In order to protect against rising health care costs, you want your nest egg to provide an income from your investment portfolio that will increase by 5% each year. Also assume that you can earn a rate of return on your investments of 8% after taxes. To receive the equivalent of $185,900 at the beginning of year 20 and at the beginning of each year thereafter for a ten-year period, each successive payment would be adjusted annually for inflation as illustrated in Table 8-5. Now you can determine the amount of money needed to provide you with that income until the total amount is completely consumed at the beginning of the tenth year. Each of the income payments must be discounted to reflect your ability to earn the assumed after-tax return of 8%. The following table shows the amounts received at the beginning of year 20 and at the beginning of each year thereafter with each successive payment adjusted annually for inflation (see Table 8-5).

TABLE 8-5

Year	Annual Income	Discounted Value (Annual Income X Present Value Factors)
1	$185,900	$185,900
2	195,195	180,731
3	204,955	175,708
4	215,198	170,824
5	225,961	166,081
6	237,264	161,482
7	249,125	156,999
8	261,580	152,632
9	274,667	148,403
10	288,387	144,251
	Total	$1,643,011

You would need an investment portfolio of $1,643,011 to provide an initial payment of $185,900 with each additional annual payment adjusted for inflation until the total portfolio is entirely dissipated in the tenth year. Now assume that you are 47 years of age and you plan to retire at the age of 67. You can now determine how much you will need to save through personal investments to accumulate a nest egg of $1,643,011 to self-fund potential expenses.

You will need an investment portfolio of approximately $1,643,011.

In this case, you will need to invest $35,903 at the end of each year for 20 years.

$1,643,011 divided by 45.7620 (see Appendix C for the appropriate divisor).

What kind of fund would you need? Complete the following paragraphs and tables with the assumptions you are using to self-fund potential expenses:

If you are still working, how long do expect to save for long-term care? _____

If you expect to continue working, you can determine how much you will need to save through personal investments to accumulate the amount needed.

I want to receive the equivalent of $ _____ at the beginning of each year for a _____ year period (to pay for required services). In order to retain my purchasing power, I want the income from my investment portfolio to increase annually with rising health care costs. I can expect that this increase will average _____% and my assumed target rate of return on my investments will be _____% after taxes. To receive the equivalent of $ _____ at the beginning of each year, each successive payment would be adjusted annually for inflation as illustrated in Table 8-6.

You can now determine the amount of money needed to provide you with that income until the total amount is entirely exhausted at the beginning of the_____ year. Each of the income payments in the previous table must be discounted to reflect your ability to earn the assumed after-tax return of _____%. The following table shows the amounts received at the beginning of each of the next _____ years, discounted annually for the after-tax return on your investment portfolio (see Table 8-7).

TABLE 8-6

Year	Annual Income ($_____X Future Value Factor)	Year	Annual Income ($_____X Future Value Factor)
1	$_____	26	$_____
2	$_____	27	$_____
3	$_____	28	$_____
4	$_____	29	$_____
5	$_____	30	$_____
6	$_____	31	$_____
7	$_____	32	$_____
8	$_____	33	$_____
9	$_____	34	$_____
10	$_____	35	$_____
11	$_____	36	$_____
12	$_____	37	$_____
13	$_____	38	$_____
14	$_____	39	$_____
15	$_____	40	$_____
16	$_____	41	$_____
17	$_____	42	$_____
18	$_____	43	$_____
19	$_____	44	$_____
20	$_____	45	$_____
21	$_____	46	$_____
22	$_____	47	$_____
23	$_____	48	$_____
24	$_____	49	$_____
25	$_____	50	$_____

I would need an investment portfolio of $_____ to provide an initial payment of $_____ with each additional annual payment adjusted for inflation until the total portfolio is completely consumed in the _____ year. I am _____ years of age, the value of my current portfolio earmarked for long-term care expenses is $_____ and I plan to save for _____ years. I can now determine how much I will need to save through personal investments to accumulate what I will need.

T A B L E   8-7

Year	Annual Income	Discounted Values (Annual Income X Present Value Factors)	Year	Annual Income	Discounted Values (Annual Income X Present Value Factors)
1	$_____	$_____	16	$_____	$_____
2	$_____	$_____	17	$_____	$_____
3	$_____	$_____	18	$_____	$_____
4	$_____	$_____	19	$_____	$_____
5	$_____	$_____	20	$_____	$_____
6	$_____	$_____	21	$_____	$_____
7	$_____	$_____	22	$_____	$_____
8	$_____	$_____	23	$_____	$_____
9	$_____	$_____	24	$_____	$_____
10	$_____	$_____	25	$_____	$_____
11	$_____	$_____	26	$_____	$_____
12	$_____	$_____	27	$_____	$_____
13	$_____	$_____	28	$_____	$_____
14	$_____	$_____	29	$_____	$_____
15	$_____	$_____	30	$_____	$_____

I will need an investment portfolio of approximately $_____.

The value of my current savings is projected to increase to $_____ in _____ years.

I will need to accumulate an additional $_____ within _____ years.

In this case, I will need to invest $_____ at the end of each year for _____ years.

$_____ (additional accumulation) divided by_____ (see Appendix C for the appropriate divisor)

How does the total amount of savings needed compare to the cost of a long-term care insurance policy? Table 8-8 compares the cost of a long-term care insurance policy to the personal investment needed to self-fund expenses by our hypothetical 47-year old.

TABLE 8-8

	Long Term Care Insurance Policy	
Year	Insurance Premium	Personal Savings
1	$2,783	$35,903
2	2,783	35,903
3	2,783	35,903
4	2,783	35,903
5	2,783	35,903
6	2,783	35,903
7	2,783	35,903
8	2,783	35,903
9	2,783	35,903
10	2,783	35,903
11	2,783	35,903
12	2,783	35,903
13	2,783	35,903
14	2,783	35,903
15	2,783	35,903
16	2,783	35,903
17	2,783	35,903
18	2,783	35,903
19	2,783	35,903
20	2,783	35,903
Total	$55,660	$718,060

Generally, the total premium paid for a policy would be substantially less than the personal savings needed to provide adequate protection making the saving option exceedingly difficult for many people.

What if you do not incur long-term care expenses after all? After all those years of paying for the insurance coverage, you get nothing in return. This is not entirely true. Over the twenty years of paying insurance premiums, you had the peace of mind in knowing that you could:

- Protect your retirement portfolio and other assets from depletion.

- Maintain your standard of living.

- Maintain your independence.

- Be able to afford the services needed.

- Avoid dependence on family or government programs.

- Leave an estate to your family.

What about the money you spent on insurance premiums? You could even implement advanced planning strategies to get back the entire amount paid for the insurance over the years. It all depends on your objectives and what you wish to accomplish.

Life Insurance

A review of your balance sheet might reveal life insurance policies that are no longer needed. Your original need for the life insurance protection may have expired. For example, the typical reason for acquiring life insurance in the pre-retirement years is to provide income protection in the event of an untimely death. Maybe the beneficiary of the policy is deceased or no longer needs the protection. After retirement, life insurance is typically needed for transfer expenses, and to pay income, inheritance and estate taxes. If the estate tax consequences lessen due to estate shrinkage or changing tax laws, the need for the life insurance may dissipate. Perhaps the premiums of the original policy are no longer affordable. Whatever the reason, a thorough analysis of ones specific situation might reveal that the insurance coverage is not needed for its original purpose. In this case, it might make sense to sell the policy. If you are over the age of 65, you should determine whether you have one or more life insurance policies that are no longer needed. As an alternative to either letting a policy lapse or surrendering the policy to the insurance company for the cash surrender value, one may receive more by liquidating the policy in the secondary market. This relatively new financial tool is called a life settlement. A life settlement is not the same as a viatical settlement, the latter of which refers to the sale of policies by terminally ill patients with life expectancies of one or two years. Life settlement firms specialize in the purchase of existing life insurance policies from insured's who are not terminally ill but may have experienced an adverse change in health since purchasing the policy. Life expectancies in this case may range anywhere from two to 15 years. After the sale, life settlement firms continue making the premium payments on the policy for the rest of the insured's life. Investors in these insurance policies receive a return on the amounts paid for policies. The appraised value of a policy depends on the insured's age, medical condition and policy details, such as the face amount, cash surrender value and outstanding policy loans. Before a life settlement firm considers purchasing a policy, the typical policy owner must:

1) Be over age 65.

2) Own a policy with a face value over $250,000.

3) Have experienced an adverse change in health since the policy was purchased.

4) Have a life expectancy of between two to 15 years.

Before an individual considers selling a policy, the policy owner should:

1) Be sure the policy really is no longer "needed."

2) Have an analysis prepared valuing a life settlement offer showing the advantages and disadvantages of retaining the policy versus the advantages and disadvantages of selling the policy.

3) Obtain offers from several life settlement firms.

4) Not do business with life settlement firms who sell policies to investors who receive personal identifying information.

For those who no longer "want" their policies, funds from the sale of an unneeded insurance policy can be a valuable resource used to pay for long-term care expenses. Additionally, the funds can be invested to supplement or enhance ones income in retirement. The following is a list of reasons why one may no longer "want" their policies:

1) Inability to continue making premium payments. The premiums have gone up over the years and are no longer affordable.

2) Original need for risk management has expired – no longer need the income protection for spouse and/or young children.

3) No longer need life insurance to pay transfer and estate taxes.

4) Funds are needed to pay for medical or long-term care expenses.

5) Funds are needed to supplement retirement income.

6) Too many individual policies.

The secondary market for life insurance policies exists so that life settlement firms can earn a rate of return ranging from 12% to 15%. This return potential is made possible due to a change in the health of an insured since the policy was originally purchased. A decline in health represents a mortality arbitrage based on the shorter life expectancy of the insured. The expectation that the insured will not live as long provides a return on investment to the life settlement firm. Since life settlement firms are acting in their own best interest when making offers to purchase life insurance policies, prospective sellers should seek qualified advice to help them evaluate a life settlement offer.

Tax consequences are another issue to consider if selling a policy is a decision one chooses to make. When a policy is sold, the seller may have to pay capital gains tax on the amount received over and above the cash value and ordinary income tax on the difference between the cash value and the cost basis. For example, suppose a seller was offered $750,000 for a $3.5 million policy. If the cost basis is $100,000 and the cash value is $185,000, the seller may have to pay capital gains tax on $565,000 and ordinary income tax on $85,000.

Finally, those considering the possibility of selling a life insurance policy should be aware of regulations in their state pertaining to the sale of insurance policies.

Consultation

Ultimately, you will need to determine your particular needs and wishes. Based on the complexity of your individual financial situation, it may be advisable to consult with a CERTIFIED FINANCIAL PLANNER™ practitioner, attorney, and/or accountant for professional advice and to discuss other options suitable for your specific situation.

Summary

There are many ways to plan a successful retirement and still protect your assets from long-term care expenses.

Since the probability of developing conditions that require long-term care increases with age, the decision to buy long-term care insurance has become an important financial planning issue.

With the passage of the Health Insurance Portability and Accountability Act in 1996, it became clearer that the government would not be paying for care in any significant way in the future. It is a clear message from Congress that long-term care insurance is important.

Self-insuring poses the challenge of acquiring a nest egg equal to the total benefits of a long-term care insurance policy. Are you confident that your accumulations for retirement will be sufficient to provide an inflation-adjusted income for as long as you live in addition to the out-of-pocket costs of an unanticipated illness or chronic condition that could require long-term health care?

References

[1] U.S. Census Bureau.
[2] U.S. Department of Health & Human Services.
[3] 2004 MetLife Market Survey of Nursing Home and Home Care Costs.

Long Term Care Insurance
- Increase coverage on MetLife policy? Buy supplemental policy?
  (P.129)

Life Insurance (P. 142)
- Cash in IBEE Policy, at retirement.
- Buy new policy (IBEE, AARP...) to cover any cost of estate taxes, transfers, etc.

Chapter 9

Wealth Preservation

"Put not your trust in money, but put your money in trust." –
Oliver Wendell Holmes

You may be surprised at how the value of your investment accounts and all other assets in your estate have grown over the years. As your estate grows, you should take steps to protect your retirement accounts and other assets from unnecessary taxation. As you know, your estate consists of virtually everything you own, such as life insurance policies, retirement and non-retirement accounts, your home, other real estate and all other personal property.

The chapter is all about planning your estate to protect against the risk of unnecessary taxation and other transfer expenses. Planning now will enable you to establish an efficient means to transfer more of your wealth to your heirs or to charity. With appropriate planning, you can protect yourself and your family from excessive taxes. We will be discussing two types of taxes in this chapter. The first is the income tax. The second is transfer tax.

> **Income Tax** – consumes part of your income as it is earned or it may be deferred until it is received in the form of distributions from retirement accounts.

> **Transfer Tax** – consumes part of your wealth transferred during life or after death. A transfer during life is called a gift

that may be subject to gift tax. A transfer after death may be subject to estate tax.

Planning now can reduce estate transfer costs. The first step is to identify the problem. Unless you identify these costs, you cannot do anything about them. The second step is to monitor the changes in the estate and gift tax rates over the years and take advantage of tax breaks to reduce transfer costs. Every person can transfer up to a certain amount without paying any taxes. This is called the exclusion amount.

The exclusion amount is:

$2.0 million in years 2006 to 2008

$3.5 million in years 2009

None in 2010 – Estate Tax Repealed

$1.0 million after 2010

The exclusion amount for gift tax purposes stays at $1.0 million. The third step is to determine the least expensive method for paying these costs.

Planning Your Estate

Step 1: Identify your estate transfer costs.

You can identify your estate transfer costs by completing an estate tax balance sheet. An estate tax balance sheet is much different than a typical balance sheet. With an estate tax balance sheet, you can clearly see whether you are effectively using your full-unified credit amounts. In our practice, we help our clients complete an updated estate tax balance sheet at least once each year after which we help them understand the concept of a two-share estate plan. In doing so we have a flowchart showing how their assets would currently pass—often showing the bypass trust (sometimes known as the family trust, residuary trust or the credit shelter trust) with zero assets if they do not already have a two-share estate plan or have not effectively funded it. We also discuss the problem of funding a trust when all or most of their assets are in the form of retirement plans. In the flowchart, our clients would also see their estate tax liability. If there is still an estate tax liability on the estate-planning flowchart, our clients are not done with their estate planning. There is always more that can be done. It is critical to the effectiveness of the wealth management process to aggressively use estate-planning techniques to try to maximize the assets passed down to future generations. By completing the following estate tax balance sheet, you can determine if you are effectively using your full-unified credit amounts (see Table 9-1).

Step 2:   Utilize tax breaks to reduce transfer costs.

You have probably heard about the scheduled repeal of the estate tax as part of The Economic Growth and Tax Relief Act of 2001. You may be wondering what effect, if any, this will have on your estate plan. The 2001 Act repeals the estate tax, but the repeal will not be effective until 2010 and there is a little-known tax increase that will replace the estate tax. During the transitional period, the act steadily increases the individual exemption amount from $2.0 million in 2006, 2007, and 2008 to $3.5 million in 2009. The other feature during the transitional period is a reduction in the top estate and gift tax rates until 2007 when it will be 45%. Effective after December 31, 2009, the loss of step-up income tax basis will replace the estate tax. This is known as "carryover" basis (with modifications). In most cases, this will result in an increased capital gains tax. Because of the phased-in increase of the unified credit that takes place during the transitional period, it is important to have your estate plan reviewed to ensure that it takes advantage of this increase.

TABLE 9-1

ASSETS	ESTATE TAX BALANCE SHEET				
	Assets titled in own name	Assets titled in spouses name	Assets titled jointly	Assets transferred by beneficiary designation	Total Assets
Cash/Cash Equivalents	$_____	$_____	$_____	$_____	$_____
Money Market Instruments	$_____	$_____	$_____	$_____	$_____
Annuities & Fixed Income Securities	$_____	$_____	$_____	$_____	$_____
Investments					
Common Stocks	$_____	$_____	$_____	$_____	$_____
Mutual Funds	$_____	$_____	$_____	$_____	$_____
Options, Commodities & Collectibles	$_____	$_____	$_____	$_____	$_____
Royalties & Mineral Interests	$_____	$_____	$_____	$_____	$_____
Other Investments	$_____	$_____	$_____	$_____	$_____
Retirement Plans					
	$_____	$_____	$_____	$_____	$_____
	$_____	$_____	$_____	$_____	$_____
	$_____	$_____	$_____	$_____	$_____
Qualified Plans					
	$_____	$_____	$_____	$_____	$_____
	$_____	$_____	$_____	$_____	$_____
IRA's					
	$_____	$_____	$_____	$_____	$_____
	$_____	$_____	$_____	$_____	$_____
	$_____	$_____	$_____	$_____	$_____
Closely Held Business Interest(s)	$_____	$_____	$_____	$_____	$_____
	$_____	$_____	$_____	$_____	$_____
Real Estate					
Personal Residence	$_____	$_____	$_____	$_____	$_____
Vacation Home	$_____	$_____	$_____	$_____	$_____
Personal Property					
Household Contents	$_____	$_____	$_____	$_____	$_____
Automobiles	$_____	$_____	$_____	$_____	$_____
Jewelry & Collectables	$_____	$_____	$_____	$_____	$_____
Other Personal Property	$_____	$_____	$_____	$_____	$_____
Notes Receivable	$_____	$_____	$_____	$_____	$_____
Totals	$_____	$_____	$_____	$_____	$_____

The need for estate planning will continue even if the estate tax law is ultimately repealed. While planning is often motivated by taxes, it also involves planning to provide for the protection and control over the disposition of assets. A properly designed estate plan ensures that your assets will pass to the beneficiaries you choose and in the manner that you want.

> Step 3:   Determine the best method of paying the
>   remaining costs.

Based on the size of your estate, you should determine how your heirs would pay the various taxes and transfer costs assessed. Ideally, you should evaluate your assets to assure sufficient liquidity. This book is all about securing a retirement income for life. In the process, you may accumulate significant assets in retirement accounts. As you will see, the value of retirement accounts can be completely eroded by both estate and income taxes without proper planning. The proceeds from insurance policies can preserve your wealth by 'replacing' the taxes your estate had to pay.

Retirement Planning

How often do you check your retirement plan beneficiary designations? Over the years, there have been many mergers between financial institutions. As a result of these mergers, retirement plan paperwork may not have been followed up on properly. The paperwork may not be carried over to the new financial institution. The old firm may transfer paperwork to the new firm but the new firm may use new forms and in the process, important information about beneficiary designations may not be correct. If you have a retirement account with a bank or other financial institution, you may in fact be surprised to find that your beneficiary designation form is incorrect. Worse yet, you may find that the beneficiary form is blank, meaning that your "estate" may now be your beneficiary. Maybe you've had relationships with advisors who have gone from one firm to another firm. If your advisor ever switches to a new firm, make sure the paperwork carries over and the beneficiaries are named in writing. **Get it in writing.** Ask your IRA institution (Bank, Broker or Mutual Fund Company) to send you the beneficiary forms and make sure your primary beneficiary and contingent beneficiary is named in writing. Otherwise, your estate may be your beneficiary and that is probably the worst choice of all because your estate is not a designated beneficiary and cannot extend the life of your IRA.

Are you comfortable with the beneficiary designations for your retirement plan(s)?

Have you reached age 70 ½ - which is the Required Beginning Date (RBD)?

The Required Beginning Date refers to the date when a retirement plan participant must begin taking distributions from his or her retirement account(s). For an IRA, the RBD is April 1st of the year following the year in which you turn 70 ½. For a qualified retirement plan, the RBD is the later of April 1st of the year following the year in which you turn 70 ½ or April 1st of the year following the year in which you retire. It is important to remember that you, as the IRA owner, are responsible for ensuring that you have received a distribution of at least the required minimum amount even if you have established a schedule of installment payments. If a required minimum distribution is not withdrawn by the appropriate deadline, you may be subject to a 50% IRS penalty on the amount not taken. If you have more than one traditional IRA, you must determine the required minimum distribution separately for each IRA. However, you can take the entire required minimum amount from any one or more of the IRAs. You should also note that you may need to adjust your fair market value because of outstanding transfers, rollovers, or re-characterizations at year-end when making this calculation. And remember: Failure to distribute the required minimum distribution by the RBD will result in a 50% penalty tax on the amount of the distribution that should have been distributed. The Uniform Distribution Table (see Exhibit 9-2) is the new life expectancy table to be used by all IRA owners to calculate lifetime distributions (unless your beneficiary is your spouse who is more than 10 years younger than you). In that case, you would not use this table. Instead, you would use the actual joint life expectancy of you and your spouse based on the regular joint life expectancy table. NOTE: The Uniform Distribution Table is never used by IRA beneficiaries to compute required distributions on their inherited IRA's.

TABLE 9-2

Uniform Distribution Table

Age of IRA Owner OR Plan Participant	Life Expectancy (in years)	Age of IRA Owner OR Plan Participant	Life Expectancy (in years)
70	27.4	93	9.6
71	26.5	94	9.1
72	25.6	95	8.6
73	24.7	96	8.1
74	23.8	97	7.6
75	22.9	98	7.1
76	22.0	99	6.7
77	21.2	100	6.3
78	20.3	101	5.9
79	19.5	102	5.5
80	18.7	103	5.2
81	17.9	104	4.9
82	17.1	105	4.5
83	16.3	106	4.2
84	15.5	107	3.9
85	14.8	108	3.7
86	14.1	109	3.4
87	13.4	110	3.1
88	12.7	111	2.9
89	12.0	112	2.6
90	11.4	113	2.4
91	10.8	114	2.1
92	10.2	115	1.9

Are you taking distributions from your company's retirement plan? If so, have you made the election that is most advantageous for you and your spouse? The problem with many company retirement plans is the lack of options both during retirement and after death. The minimum distribution rules allow for the payout of benefits or distributions over the beneficiary's life expectancy. These so called "stretch provisions" enable a young beneficiary to receive the benefit of continued tax deferral for many years to come. **NOTE: Qualified plans may require a lump sum distribution.** Company plans, such as any employer profit sharing, 401(k), 403(b) or other qualified plan is not required to offer a "stretch" payout over the beneficiary's life expectancy. Since they are not required to offer it, most plans do not. Many employers want to eliminate the administration of an employee's money after his or her death. So they offer the beneficiary only one form of payout: a lump sum distribution. This is fine if the beneficiary is the employee's spouse. An employee's spouse can rollover the lump sum distribution into his or her own IRA with continued income tax deferral. Not so if the beneficiary is the deceased employee's child. In this case, a child beneficiary would lose the ability to rollover the lump sum and therefore lose the continued tax deferral. You should evaluate the distribution options for any company retirement plan where you are a participant to determine whether there are any such restrictions regarding distribution options that could accelerate income taxes.

Rollover Options

If you have a vested balance in your employer's retirement plan, then you may be entitled to an eligible rollover distribution when you leave. As a general rule, you can:

1)   **Leave your vested balance in your previous employer's plan and roll it over to an IRA at a later time.** Although this option would allow for continued tax-deferred compounding, your investment choices would be limited to those offered by the plan, you cannot make additional contributions and there may be restrictions regarding distributions that may accelerate income taxes.

2) **Have it transferred directly to a rollover IRA.** This option would also allow for continued tax deferred compounding, but you would now have more investment choices without any restrictions on the way distributions would be paid out to you and your beneficiaries. You can make additional contributions, but this would preclude you from rolling this account over to a new employer's plan.

3) **Have it transferred directly to a new employers plan.** This option would allow for continued tax-deferred compounding, but there may or may not be more investment options. There may be more restrictions on your ability to access your money.

4) **Take the distribution now and pay taxes on the amount of the distribution you receive** (Note that distributions received prior to the age of 59 ½ are subject to an early withdrawal penalty – with certain exceptions). With this option, there is no more tax-deferred growth and a portion of your distribution would be consumed by taxes.

5) **Take a distribution now and roll it over into an IRA within 60 days** (subject to 20% withholding). Since the check is made out to you, 20% of the distribution is withheld to pay potential income taxes. You would have to make up this 20% difference out-of-pocket and rollover the total distribution amount within 60 days. After the rollover, you would continue to benefit from tax-deferred compounding, but with more investment choices and no restrictions on the way distributions would be paid out to you and your beneficiaries. Once again, additional contributions to this account would preclude you from rolling this account over to a new employer's plan.

6) **Purchase a qualified annuity.** With this option, tax deferral continues and distributions may not be required at age 70 ½ and you can receive an income

guaranteed for life. There is considerable variation in the types of annuities available. You should always compare the interest rates and expenses for the different annuities offered by competitive providers.

Traditional IRA

A traditional IRA may allow you to deduct contributions from your taxable income, depending on your modified adjusted gross income (MAGI) and whether you participate in a retirement plan at work. If you participate in a qualified plan at work, contributions to an IRA are deductible if MAGI does not exceed the following amounts (see Exhibit 9-1).

EXHIBIT 9-1

Contributions	Joint	Single
Fully Deductible	If MAGI < $75,000	If MAGI < $50,000
Partially Deductible	If MAGI is $75,000 to $85,000	If MAGI is $50,000 to $60,000
Not Deductible	If MAGI > $85,000	If MAGI is > $60,000

Roth IRA

The contributions to a Roth IRA are never deductible but the distributions are tax-free. Additionally, there is an income limit for making contributions to a Roth IRA (see Exhibit 9-2).

EXHIBIT 9-2

Contributions	Joint	Single
Full Contribution	If MAGI < $150,000	If MAGI < $95,000
Partial Contribution	If MAGI > $150,000 < $160,000	If MAGI > $95,000 < $110,000
No Contribution	If MAGI > $160,000	If MAGI > $110,000

Conversion To A Roth IRA

Although you cannot directly transfer your assets from your company plan to a Roth IRA, you can first transfer them to a rollover IRA and then initiate a conversion. The income limit for converting a traditional IRA to a Roth IRA is $100,000. What effect would a conversion have on the preservation of your wealth?

1) The initial conversion would be subject to income tax. Assuming one has $1.0 million invested in retirement assets, a total conversion would be taxed at the highest marginal rate of 35% (see Exhibit 9-3). Imagine writing a check for $350,000 just to pay the taxes on this distribution.

2) Although the balance is reduced by 35%, the future growth is entirely tax-free.

3) Unlike a traditional IRA, there are no required minimum distributions with a Roth IRA. With a traditional IRA, required minimum distributions are taxable starting at age 70 ½.

4) If you have more than enough income from other sources, the required minimum distributions from a traditional IRA, which are taxable, will only increase your federal income tax liability. You may not want to withdraw money from your IRA.

5) By eliminating the required minimum distribution, you would reduce your federal income taxes on the amount of the distribution. You would also reduce the taxability of your Social Security benefits. The income thresholds that determine whether Social Security benefits are taxable are based on "combined income," which is the sum of your adjusted gross income (AGI) plus nontaxable interest plus one-half your Social Security benefits as indicated in Exhibit 9-4.

EXHIBIT 9-3

2006 Tax Rate Schedule

Taxable Income ($)	Base Amount Of Tax ($)	Plus	Rate On Excess (%) (also called marginal tax rate or tax bracket)	Of The Amount Over ($)
Married filing jointly and surviving spouses				
0 to 15,100	0.00	plus	10	0
15,100 to 61,300	1,510.00	plus	15	15,100
61,300 to 123,700	8,440.00	plus	25	61,300
123,700 to 188,450	24,040.00	plus	28	123,700
188,450 to 336,550	42,170.00	plus	33	188,450
Over 336,550	91,043.00	plus	35	336,550
Single				
0 to 7,550	0.00	plus	10	0
7,550 to 30,650	755.00	plus	15	7,550
30,650 to 74,200	4,220.00	plus	25	30,650
74,200 to 154,800	15,107.50	plus	28	74,200
154,800 to 336,550	37,675.50	plus	33	154,800
Over 336,550	97,653.00	plus	35	336,550
Head of household				
0 to 10,750	0.00	plus	10	0
10,750 to 41,050	1,075.00	plus	15	10,750
41,050 to 106,000	5,620.00	plus	25	41,050
106,000 to 171,650	21,857.50	plus	28	106,000
171,650 to 336,550	40,239.50	plus	33	171,650
Over 336,550	94,656.50	plus	35	336,550
Married filing separately				
0 to 7,550	0.00	plus	10	0
7,550 to 30,650	755.00	plus	15	7,550
30,650 to 61,850	4,220.00	plus	25	30,650
61,850 to 94,225	12,020.00	plus	28	61,850
94,225, to 168,275	21,085.00	plus	33	94,225
Over 168,275	45,521.50	plus	35	168,275
Estates and trusts				
0 to 2,050	0.00	plus	15	0
2,050 to 4,850	307.50	plus	25	2,050
4,850 to 7,400	1,007.50	plus	28	4,850
7,400 to 10,050	1,721.50	plus	33	7,400
Over 10,050	2,596.00	plus	35	10,050

Source: 2006 Federal Tax Rate Schedules, IRS; 2006 Federal Tax Rates for Estates and Trusts

EXHIBIT 9-4

Amount of Social Security Subject to Tax	
Combined Income (joint)	**Combine Income (single)**
50% Between $32,000 and $44,000	Between $25,000 and $34,000
85% Over $44,000	Over $34,000

Source: Social Security Administration.

The decision about whether or not to convert your traditional IRA to a Roth IRA will depend on your goals. Will you need the money from your retirement plan for living expenses? Would you rather put off taking the required minimum distributions until some time after age 70 ½? Would you rather not take any distributions at all letting the balance grow tax-free for your heirs? You may decide that a Roth conversion is right for you, but the tax consequences are too high to bear. Remember, a total distribution all in one year may put you into a higher tax bracket subjecting you to a much higher tax burden. If so, you may consider a partial conversion of an amount that would keep you in a lower tax bracket by converting a portion of your traditional IRA to a Roth over a period of years. In lieu of a Roth conversion, you may wish to retain your traditional IRA but implement other strategies that will have the same effect of increasing your family's wealth.

Other Options

Ultimately, you will need to determine the best way to manage your retirement assets based on your particular needs and wishes. The key to making the right decision is information about the potential advantages and disadvantages of each option for your particular situation. In accordance with your objectives, a **Qualified Plan Analysis** will assist you in exploring various planning scenarios to maximize your plan for retirement. An important part of our practice is to help our clients coordinate their retirement plan, especially the distributions, into estate and financial (cash flow) planning.

We help them determine:

1) How the various distribution options affect their qualified plan accounts and IRAs.
2) The effects of stretching out their qualified plans and IRAs over multiple generations.
3) How they can defer income taxes as long as possible.

It may be advisable to consult with a CERTIFIED FINANCIAL PLANNER™ practitioner or other financial advisor if you were born before 1936 or if you have retirement plan contributions invested in company stock and to discuss other options suitable for your specific situation. For conversion options, you should have a quantitative analysis prepared showing the benefits, if any, of converting various amounts of your traditional IRA to a Roth IRA.

Estate Planning

We already discussed the importance of assuring that the beneficiary designations of your IRA's and 401(k) plans are all correct and named in writing on the appropriate beneficiary forms. Like life insurance proceeds, retirement benefits pass by beneficiary designation. So the beneficiary designation determines the disposition of your retirement assets after death – not your will or living trust.

Who is the primary beneficiary of your retirement accounts?

The primary beneficiary is the person who inherits the retirement plan after the owners death.

Who is the contingent beneficiary?

The contingent beneficiary would inherit the retirement plan only if the primary beneficiary failed to survive the owner.

At the beginning of this chapter, we discussed how you can identify your estate transfer costs by completing an estate tax balance sheet. By completing an estate tax balance sheet, you can determine if you are effectively using your full-unified credit amounts. A current estate tax balance sheet can help you understand the concept of a two-share estate plan showing how your assets would currently pass to your heirs. If you already have a two-share estate plan with a bypass trust (sometimes known as the B trust, family trust, residuary trust or the credit shelter trust), the estate tax balance sheet will show how the trust could be funded with both pre-tax and/or after-tax assets. Often, the bypass trust will show zero assets if you do not have a two-share estate plan or if you have not effectively funded it. A completed Estate Tax Worksheet will help you see if there is still an estate tax liability. It is critical to the effectiveness of the wealth management process to aggressively use estate-planning techniques to try to maximize the assets passed down to future generations.

A trust can be a fundamental part of planning for the future. Trusts can help you avoid unnecessary taxes, put your wealth to use in exactly the way you wish, accumulate assets for retirement or your beneficiaries and much more. For example, a living trust is a legal agreement under which a trustee manages certain assets for your benefit or for the benefit of another person or persons during your lifetime. A living trust has become popular for many reasons.

- A living trust can facilitate management of your assets in the event of your incapacity. Since assets held in the name of the trust are free from probate, there is nothing to probate (the probate process can consume as much as 10% of your estate).

- You can place just about any type of property in a living trust, and either withdraw or reinvest all of the income generated by trust assets during your lifetime. Since a living trust is a private agreement, information concerning the contents remains private.

- The flexibility of a living trust makes it ideal for a wide range of individuals, including those who have dependents with special needs, are marrying for the second time, or who want to provide effective pre-nuptial protection for their children.

Bypass Trust

The bypass trust (sometimes known as the B trust, family trust, residuary trust or the credit shelter trust) is used by a married couple so they both can take advantage of each exemption from estate taxes. Without this trust, the entire estate from the first to die usually passes to the survivor tax-free (due to the unlimited marital deduction). At the death of the remaining spouse, only one exemption amount is available to reduce the transfer costs assessed upon the death of that person.

Are your retirement accounts a significant part of your estate in relation to your other assets?

If your retirement accounts are disproportionate in size to your assets, the combined income and estate tax consequences could be devastating unless you do the proper planning. The following example illustrates how large these tax consequences can be. Consider the estate of a married couple with a $4.0 million IRA owned by one of them, a home worth $500,000 owned jointly and few other assets. Suppose the spouse is named primary beneficiary and the children are named contingent beneficiaries of the IRA. After the IRA owner dies, the spouse will inherit the $4.0 million IRA, the $500,000 home and other assets. The estate for estate tax purposes is $4.5 million. Due to the unlimited marital deduction, virtually all transfers to a surviving spouse are tax-free. The property must be included in the decedent's gross estate and actually pass to the surviving spouse to qualify. For the purposes of this illustration, assume the estate is still $4.5 million when the property transfers to the children after the death of the surviving spouse. In the year 2006, the estate tax exclusion amount is $2.0 million. This means that the remaining $2.5 million is potentially subject to federal estate tax at the rate of 46%, which amounts to a staggering $1,150,000 ($2.5 million X 0.46%). Where will the tax money come from to pay the federal estate tax that is due within nine months after death? Assuming the house could be sold within nine months, up to $500,000 may be available there. The other $650,000 could come from the IRA. A withdrawal of $650,000 from the IRA in one year would push one into the highest tax bracket of 35% plus any state tax. Assuming a combined federal and state tax rate of 40%, the total income tax due on the $650,000 IRA distribution is $260,000 ($650,000 X 0.40). Where will the tax money come from to pay the federal and state income taxes that are due by April 15th of the year following death? The IRA, of course. A withdrawal of $260,000 from the IRA would be taxed at a combined rate of up to 40%, or $104,000 ($260,000 X 0.40). Where will the $104,000 come from to pay the combined taxes due? Another $41,600 is owed in federal and state taxes. So far, 35% or $1,555,600 of the estate has been consumed in paying estate and income taxes as illustrated below.

Original Estate Value	$4,500,000
Less: Exclusion Amount	$2,000,000
Balance	$2,500,000
Less: Federal Estate Tax	$1,150,000
Less: Income Taxes	$ 405,600
Total Estate & Income Taxes	$1,555,600

This unfortunate outcome could have been avoided by planning ahead with a qualified practitioner. In the above illustration, the value of retirement assets was disproportionately large in relation to the total estate. As such, the house and the IRA were the only assets available to pay the estate and income taxes. Although the house was sold to provide a portion of the needed funds, a large percentage of the IRA was eventually liquidated to pay the rest. With proper planning, the entire estate could have been preserved for the beneficiaries or heirs.

Individual Retirement Trust

Individuals with large accumulations in IRAs may wish to preserve these and other tax favored accounts for their beneficiaries by naming an "Individual Retirement Trust" or "IRA trust" as beneficiary rather than naming a person directly on the beneficiary designation form. Naming a trust as beneficiary provides control over distributions after the IRA owner's death. This may be important for several reasons.

1) **One or more beneficiaries may be minors**. A minor child is simply too young to manage significant financial assets.

2) **The beneficiary may be disabled or incompetent.**

3) **The beneficiary may be irresponsible with money.** Note: With a person beneficiary, such as a child or grandchild, the retirement assets become the property of the beneficiary after the account owner's death.

4) **To assure that beneficiaries from a previous marriage receive their inheritance.**

5) **In most states, distributions to a designated beneficiary – exclusive of a trust usually avoid probate through beneficiary designations included in retirement plan contracts.** In some states, retirement assets may be subject to the probate process. With an Individual Retirement Trust, assets would pass according to the terms of the trust in lieu of the probate process.

6) **For asset protection.** State statutes may provide judgment protection from creditor claims against non-

grantor beneficiaries of a trust. This can lengthen the protection term of the plan over their life expectancy, by virtue of restricting a beneficiary's right to make lump-sum withdrawals from a retirement account.

Under the Comprehensive Retirement Security and Pension Reform Act of 2001, retirement plan owners may implement new strategies with trusts by virtue of the new recalculation rules. Providing certain IRS requirements are met, plan owners may now use remarkable multigenerational planning strategies by allowing a trustee to receive minimum distributions on behalf of a plan beneficiary. In order for a trust to qualify as a designated beneficiary and satisfy the qualifying terms prescribed under Treasury Regulations Section 1.401(a)(9)-4, A-5., as a designated beneficiary trust (DBT):

1) The trust must be valid under state law.
2) The trust must be irrevocable at death.
3) The beneficiaries of the trust must be identifiable.
4) A copy of the trust instrument must be provided to the plan administrator by October 31st of the year following the IRA owner's death.

Trusts offer a combination of versatility and planning capabilities not otherwise available for the retirement plan owner with custodial IRAs. Plan owners may now impose certain post mortem restrictions on withdrawal rights by combining the minimum distribution requirements with creative estate planning techniques to alleviate any concern that a 'spendthrift' beneficiary may withdraw large amounts all at once. Additionally, spouses and children may not know that there are specific rules for receiving retirement plan distributions. Wealthy families have used trusts for many years to preserve wealth by preventing their children from squandering the family fortune in one fell swoop. If drafted properly, the plan administrator will be allowed to "see through the trustee" for the purposes of making all retirement plan distributions payable to the trust. We already discussed the importance of checking your retirement plan beneficiary designations and to make sure they are correct and named in writing. An estate is not a beneficiary. A beneficiary who inherits an IRA through an estate will not be able to extend the life of the IRA over his or her life expectancy. Only individuals named on a beneficiary designation form can extend distributions over his or her life expectancy. A trust is not a beneficiary unless it qualifies as a "see through trust." If the trust qualifies, the trustee could take advantage of the favorable MDRs for the purposes of making only the minimum required distributions to the trust's beneficiaries.

Trust planning with retirement accounts is primarily about the post-mortem control that a trust grantor can obtain, especially now in light of the see through allowances that can be used in combination with the new MDR recalculation options. Through discreet planning, a trust can impose age-based allocation restrictions over a retirement plan in tandem with the current MDRs adjusting them as children age and mature financially. Such planning strategies can fulfill a plan owner's desire for post-mortem control using payout provisions that will "enforce" the minimal withdrawal terms allowed under the MDRs. If a longer withdrawal period can be applied to a retirement account, the funds will obviously realize tax-deferred accumulations for a longer period if the money stays in the account. Of course, the longer money stays in the account growing tax-deferred, the more the account may ultimately be worth to the beneficiary.

As with any planning strategy, trust planning should be integrated with other aspects of your financial plan. As such, you should consult with qualified professionals to make sure any trust is in compliance with the terms of the Treasury Regulations and also that your beneficiaries receive the most favorable distribution options.

Private Annuity Trust

As you know, one way of managing longevity risk is by converting a portion of your investment portfolio into a ***commercial*** annuity. A commercial annuity is a contract with an insurance company. In return for a lump sum payment or a series of payments, an insurance company will make periodic payments to the annuitant guaranteed to last for life or for some other period certain. A *private* annuity is a contract between two parties who could be individuals, trusts or business entities. One party essentially transfers assets having a certain value as of a specific date to another party who agrees to make periodic payments to the other party for the rest of their life or for some other period of time. In Chapter 7, we showed how the role of a commercial annuity was to provide protection against outliving one's money in retirement. It is an income distribution technique for providing protection against the longevity risk. A private annuity is a wealth preservation technique used to transfer assets to the next generation on a tax- favored basis. There are many advantages to using a private annuity trust as described below:

1) To remove assets from ones estate thereby reducing the estate for transfer tax purposes.
2) To convert a non-income producing asset into a stream of income.
3) To defer capital gains tax on a highly appreciated asset.

In each case, the transferor receives a stream of fixed income payments for the rest of his or her life or for the life of both husband and wife, as would be the case with a joint and last survivor annuity. With highly appreciated assets, for example, a large capital gain would be realized all in one year if the property were sold outright. If, however, the property were exchanged for an annuity, only a portion of the capital gain would be taxed each year over the life of the contract. The total annuity payments received by the annuitant, or transferor, each year would consist of capital gains, ordinary income and basis. The portion representing a return of capital is not taxed. A private annuity trust can be used to transfer many types of highly appreciated assets, such as equity investments, business interests and real estate. A private annuity trust is an especially attractive technique to use for non-income producing real estate, such as undeveloped land. In this case, large imbedded capital gains can make selling the property undesirable. The realization of capital gains all in one year can be costly for income tax purposes. Avoiding the sale of highly appreciated assets can also be costly for estate tax purposes. Now, one can reduce the size of his or her estate and spread the income tax consequences out over a number of years and receive a stream of income for life on what otherwise may have been a non-income producing asset. For those with multimillion-dollar estates, this strategy can allow families to transfer property worth well over the $11,000 annual gift tax exclusion on to the next generation now without excessive tax consequences. Their family may also benefit from potentially lower transfer tax costs in the future.

One disadvantage of a private annuity in comparison to a commercial annuity relates to security. One may feel more secure about entering into a long-term contract with a reputable insurance company as opposed to a single individual. The transferor must feel confident in the transferee's ability to make the payments on an individual level for many years into the future. Since the transfer of property is irrevocable, the annuitant cannot retrieve their property if the transferee defaults. A disadvantage from the transferee's perspective relates to longevity. Since the transferee is obligated to make payments for the annuitant's lifetime, there is the uncertainty about how long that may be. If the annuitant lives for a very long time, the transferee may wind up paying much more than they expected for the property.

Like any other advanced wealth preservation strategy or technique, there are usually certain requirements that must be complied with. For example, to avoid the immediate recognition of capital gains all in one year, the annuity payments cannot be secured by the transferred property. Someone who is terminally ill cannot use a private annuity arrangement to execute a transfer. Additionally, there must be an accurate assessment of value derived at the time of the of the transfer. This is particularly important for hard-to-value assets, including real estate and closely held business interests. If necessary, a qualified appraiser should be engaged for these assets.

As always, a qualified advisor with experience in this subject should be consulted regarding the suitability of this technique.

Basis Planning

As we described in the last section on the Private Annuity Trust, many people will avoid selling a highly appreciated asset since a large capital gain could be realized on the sale. For those with low basis assets, decisions about whether to gift or bequeath them have been made more complicated than ever due in part to changes in the federal exemption amount and the scheduled repeal of the estate tax as part of the Economic Growth and Tax Relief Act of 2001. Basis planning involves the effective application of the transfer tax rules concerning cost basis to reduce estate transfer costs – income or estate tax. For years, those with large estates have been able to utilize trusts and other advanced wealth preservation strategies like those described in this chapter to reduce or avoid estate taxes entirely. With the increase in the exclusion amount over the years and the possible repeal of the estate tax altogether in 2010, the focus is starting to shift to the potential income tax consequences of one's estate and the potential for state estate taxation as well. For some people, they will be worse off with a complete repeal of the estate tax. As stated earlier, effective December 31, 2009, the loss of step-up income tax basis will replace the estate tax. This is known as "carry-over" basis. In most cases, this will result in an increased capital gains tax. Consider the scenario of a person who dies owning a $10 million office building with a tax basis of $0 and a loan on the property in the amount of $8.5 million. Prior to December 31, 2009, the property bequeathed to a son or daughter would receive the date of death fair market value (FMV) or step-up income tax basis of $10 million. The child could sell the property for $10 million and owe no capital gains tax. After December 31, 2009, the property bequeathed to a son or daughter will receive a carryover basis (with modifications; $1.3 million general basis increase with an additional $3 million basis increase for property left to a spouse). In this case, the child cannot sell the building because after paying off the mortgage, there are insufficient proceeds left to pay the income taxes.

FMV Date of Sale	$10,000,000
Less: Carryover Basis	$ 1,300,000
Taxable Gain	$ 8,700,000
Capital Gains Taxes	$ 2,175,000

Summary

Gross Proceeds	$10,000,000
Less: Mortgage	$ 8,500,000
Less: Income Tax	$ 2,175,000
Short	$ 675,000

Prior to possible repeal of the estate tax, similar calculations would show whether it is more advantageous to leave assets in one's estate so the heirs receive a step-up basis or remove the assets from one's estate by gifting the assets so the heirs receive a carryover basis. Once again, prior to the scheduled repeal of the estate tax, heirs receive a step-up income tax basis for property bequeathed to them versus a carryover basis for property received as a gift. Consider the scenario of an individual who dies owning $2 million in stock with a basis of $100,000. If the stock is bequeathed to a son or daughter, the child will receive a step-up income tax basis of $2 million. The child could sell the stock and owe no capital gains tax. On the other hand, if the stock is gifted to a son or daughter, the child will receive a carryover basis of $100,000. If the child sells the stock for $2 million, the capital gains tax will be $285,000 ($1,900,000 X 0.15). Likewise, if the individual owning the $2 million stock with a basis of $100,000 sells the stock during life, the capital gains tax will be the same $285,000. In this scenario, the capital gains tax rate is 15%. In the process of determining which assets to leave in the estate and which assets to gift, it makes sense to compare the income and estate tax rates in effect at the time. In 2006, the top estate rate is 46% compared to the highest capital gains rate of 15% (25% if depreciation recapture). If leaving the $2 million stock in the estate subjects the estate to the top rate of 46%, a more acceptable alternative would be to implement a gifting strategy to remove the stock from the estate (15% versus 46% rate). If leaving the $2 million stock in the estate would not result in estate tax due to the estate tax exclusion, a more acceptable alternative may be to bequeath the stock. In the latter case, the step-up income tax basis will result in significant tax savings for the heirs of the estate.

It also makes sense to compare the capital gains rate for different taxpayers. Consider the scenario in which an individual wishes to transfer stock to a lower bracket family member. This transfer may result in tax savings due to the difference in tax rates (5% versus 15%). A married couple could gift up to $24,000 worth of stock without having to file a gift tax return (annual gift tax exclusion is $12,000 in 2006). Assume the basis of the stock is $5,000. If the parents sell the stock, the capital gains tax will be $2,850 ($19,000 X 0.15). If the child sells the stock, the capital gains tax would be $950 ($19,000 X 0.05). If the gift exceeds the annual gift tax exclusion, the parents would have to file a gift tax return. However, a gift tax would not be due unless their total lifetime gifts exceed $1 million.

For those with high basis assets, a decision about whether to gift or bequeath them depends on the fair market value (FMV) of the assets at death. As stated earlier, inherited property receives a FMV basis (date of death value) for income tax purposes. Consider a scenario in which an individual wishes to transfer $50,000 in stock with a basis of $55,000. If the stock is bequeathed to a son or daughter, the child will actually receive a step-down income tax basis of $50,000 (date of death FMV). If the child sells the stock, he or she will not be able to report a loss for income tax purposes. If the individual owning the stock sells the stock during life, the realized capital loss of $5,000 ($50,000 sell price less $55,000 cost basis) could be used to offset up to $5,000 of capital gains or up to $3,000 in other income. Any unused loss can be carried forward to the next tax year. In general, it is preferable for a higher bracket individual to sell higher basis assets in order to utilize capital losses (if any).

As with the Private Annuity Trust, there must be an accurate assessment of value derived at the time of the transfer. It is relatively easy to obtain values for marketable securities. But with hard to value assets, such as real estate and closely held business interests, it is particularly important to obtain an accurate assessment of value. If necessary, a qualified appraiser should be engaged for these assets. Like so many other strategies discussed in this book, the most acceptable alternative will depend on each person's circumstances and goals.

Life Insurance

During the accumulation and protection stage of your life, life insurance is used to protect against loss of income until assets are sufficient to meet the needs of your family. During the distribution and preservation stage of life, your need for life insurance may continue, especially if the value of your assets exceed the federal estate tax equivalent exemption.

Life insurance is perhaps the most commonly used estate liquidity source. The major purpose of life insurance is to preserve wealth by providing the cash needed to pay estate, income and other transfer expenses. If life insurance is mistakenly left in the wrong form of ownership, however, unnecessary taxes may be imposed on the proceeds. As you may know, proceeds from a life insurance policy are free of income tax to the beneficiary. However, the proceeds are subject to estate tax if you retain any of the following "incidences of ownership:"

1) You are the owner of the policy.
2) You pay the premium.
3) You have the right to borrow from the cash value in the policy.
4) You can name and change the beneficiary.
5) You are the applicant.

If you retain any of these "incidences of ownership," the proceeds of the policy would be included in your estate for estate tax purposes. Therefore, most individuals with large insurance policies or estates that exceed the federal estate tax equivalent exemption will remove these policies from their estate. By establishing an Insurance Trust, the insurance proceeds will be accessible for paying transfer taxes without being included as part of the estate.

In the previous example of the $4.5 million estate, over $1.5 million was consumed by estate and income taxes. The most important reason for using insurance to pay estate taxes is to assure that assets will not have to be liquidated to pay these costs. Additionally, for people with large estates, especially those with large retirement assets, the least expensive way to pay estate and income taxes is with insurance.

What To Do Now

You should immediately do some IRA distribution planning, which includes estate and income tax planning for your retirement accounts. The planning process addressed in this chapter is:

1) Choose the proper beneficiaries for each of your retirement plans.
2) Evaluate the distribution options for company plans.
3) Evaluate the rollover options for your company plans.

4) Make sure that your beneficiary designations and distribution methods are coordinated with your overall estate plan.

5) Identify your estate transfer costs.

6) Because of the phased-in increase of the unified credit that takes place during the transitional period, it is important to have your estate plan reviewed periodically to ensure that it takes advantage of this increase.

7) If the estate tax law is ultimately repealed, it will be important to have a plan for passing assets to your beneficiaries in a way that will take into account the potential income taxes your heirs may incur should they sell assets received from you.

8) Utilize tax breaks to reduce transfer costs.

9) Determine the best method of paying these costs.

10) Identify circumstances under which you may use one or more of the advanced wealth preservation techniques described in this chapter.

Other Options

The need for estate planning will continue even if the estate tax law is ultimately repealed. While planning is often motivated by taxes, it also involves planning to provide for the protection and control over the disposition of assets. A properly designed estate plan ensures that your assets will pass to the beneficiaries you choose, and in the manner that you want. Ultimately, you will need to express your own wishes regarding the transfer of your assets to your heirs and have your plan reviewed periodically to determine whether your living trust, ancillary documents such as a durable power of attorney, living will and durable power of attorney for health care (or designation of health care surrogate) and other wealth preservation vehicles need updated based on changes in personal circumstances and/or tax laws.

We highly recommend that you consult with a CERTIFIED FINANCIAL PLANNER™ practitioner, attorney, accountant and/or other financial advisor for competent advice and to discuss other options available for your specific situation.

Leaving a Legacy

Estate planning is about much more than just money. A recent study found that money was ranked last in a list of estate planning issues.[1] More important issues like sharing values and life lessons, understanding final instructions and wishes, and distributing personal assets – especially those with emotional meaning and value were ranked well ahead of money. Leaving a "legacy" - including family values, traditions and history is becoming a more important topic of discussion. Having in depth conversations with children and grandchildren about the past, sharing stories and traditions and passing on family values can be so much more important and meaningful than discussions about financial issues. Ask yourself one question, How would you like to be remembered? Would you rather be remembered as a loving and caring person? Would you like to be remembered for your honesty and integrity? Do you want to be remembered for your trustworthiness, your compassion, by being a good listener or as a good teacher? Having conversations with loved ones about your life stories can be some of the most meaningful times in life. In addition to wealth transfer, a true legacy includes memories and the lessons and values that you teach to your children over a lifetime. It is becoming increasingly common for people to express their values and traditions in writing as part of their estate plan. I especially think that legacy planning provides a great opportunity for people to write a book for future generations passing on their values and beliefs for many years to come.

References

[1] AgeWave Research and Consulting; Allianz American Legacies Study.

Chapter Notes

IRA Minimum Distribution—
- Must begin by April 1 of the year following the year you turn 70 ½ (by 4/1/28). Check Required minimum distribution amounts. Determine Required minimum distribution separately for each IRA. (P. 152)

401(k)— No early withdrawal penalty (10%) after age 59 ½ (5/10/16). Still must pay income tax. (P. 155)

Social Security Income Tax — (2006) 85% of SSA benefits are taxed, if combined income is > $44K. (P. 159)

Estate Planning
- Monitor estate tax exclusion amounts (p. 148). If estate value might exceed exclusion amount, then consult with Estate Attorney
- Add IRA's to trust?

Chapter 10

Choosing a Financial Advisor

"He that won't be counseled can't be helped."
– Benjamin Franklin

U ltimately, you will need to determine your particular financial needs and wishes. With information abundant and readily available, you could opt to go it alone. It can be very challenging, however, to do the specific financial analysis and investment research needed to secure your financial well being for the long term. In 2004, findings from a Retirement Readiness & Middle America Survey revealed that 65% of Americans do not know what their monthly budget should be after retirement and have not planned to collect a "retirement paycheck."[1] In addition, the study showed clear signs that people need to focus beyond saving to more comprehensive planning. Based on the complexity of your individual financial situation, it may be advisable to consult with a CERTIFIED FINANCIAL PLANNER™ practitioner, attorney, accountant or other advisor for professional advice and to discuss the investment strategies and other options suitable for your specific situation. Deciding to work with a financial advisor may be one of the most important decisions you make for yourself and your loved ones. After reading this book, you should understand that financial planning is a 'process' of determining how individuals can achieve their goals for tomorrow by coordinating and managing today's financial decisions. It is a personal, interactive, process driven approach for solving complex financial problems.

Statistics show that 74% of people nearing retirement would prefer to consult with a professional financial advisor for reliable advice on retirement planning decisions.[2] But as more and more people call themselves "financial advisors" or "financial planners," how do you find the right professional to help you address your unique financial planning needs? You may be confused about how to distinguish one "financial advisor" or "financial planner" from another. The words "financial advisor" and "financial planner" have almost become generic terms used by a multitude of firms offering financial services. Unfortunately, this confusion leads many people to choose firms who are primarily product driven, with more of an interest in selling you financial products, such as investments and insurance, rather than providing reliable advice. You really need to take your time when choosing a financial professional. Are you looking for a financial planner who will put your needs and interests first and provide guidance for all of your financial decisions over the course of your lifetime? Are you looking for someone who can help you build, manage and preserve your wealth through objective planning? Are you looking for someone who is service oriented – not sales oriented?

Credentials

As the number of people seeking financial advice continues to grow, it is important to know how to identify qualified financial planning professionals committed to competent and ethical behavior. Advisors who aspire to provide true wealth management services have typically taken steps to complete an educational course of study at a college or university after which they must pass comprehensive examinations that test their financial planning knowledge. For example, candidates for the CFP® designation must have a minimum of three years experience in the financial planning process in addition to the education and examination requirements described above prior to earning the right to use the CFP® marks. The CFP® marks are owned by the Certified Financial Planner Board of Standards, Inc. and are awarded to individuals who successfully complete CFP

Board's initial and ongoing certification requirements.[3] CFP®
practitioners must also agree to abide by the following Code of Ethics
agreeing to provide their clients with objective financial planning
advice and services.

Code of Ethics

Principle 1 - Integrity

A CFP® designee shall offer and provide professional services
with integrity.

Principle 2 - Objectivity

A CFP® designee shall be objective in providing professional
services to clients.

Principle 3 - Competence

A CFP® designee shall provide services to clients competently
and maintain the necessary knowledge and skill to continue
to do so in those areas in which the designee is engaged.

Principle 4 - Fairness

A CFP® designee shall perform professional services in a
manner that is fair and reasonable to clients, principals,
partners, and employers and shall disclose conflicts of interest in providing such services.

Principle 5 - Confidentiality

A CFP® designee shall not disclose any confidential client information without the specific consent of the client unless in

response to proper legal process, to defend against charges of wrongdoing by the CFP® designee or in connection with a civil dispute between the CFP® designee and client.

Principle 6 – Professionalism

A CFP® designee's conduct in all matters shall reflect credit upon the profession.

Principle 7 – Diligence

A CFP® designee shall act diligently in providing professional services.

Source: Certified Financial Planner Board of Standards, Inc.

CFP® practitioners must also follow certain standards – based on Financial Planning Practice Standards – which describe the process used during a financial planning engagement. The following six-step process will help you understand what to expect from the financial planning process:

The Financial Planning Process

1. Establishing and defining the client-planner relationship. A CFP® practitioner will define the scope of the engagement, clearly explain and document the services to be provided, the method of compensation and other relevant information.

2. Gathering client data including goals. A CFP® practitioner will work to identify your needs, objectives and risk tolerances and your time horizon for achieving your goals.

3.   Analyzing and evaluating your financial status. Practice Standards also require a CFP® practitioner to gather and review all necessary financial data when designing and implementing a plan to help you reach your goals.

4.   Developing and presenting financial planning recommendations.

5.   Implementing the financial planning recommendations.

6.   Monitoring the financial planning recommendations. Once a plan is in place, it needs to be monitored, reviewed and updated to meet dynamic circumstances.

Registration of Financial Planners

In the process of providing financial planning and wealth management services, a qualified advisor should begin with a thorough understanding of your current situation and future needs. The typical examination should include discussions with you about risk and return statistics for managed assets and a discussion of capital market theory. Based on the information gathered above, the investment advisor should illustrate his or her investment process, philosophy and methods of portfolio design. A comprehensive level of planning should include the development of a specific Investment Proposal and Investment Policy Statement (IPS) that provides a paper trail of policies, practices and procedures for investment decision. These policies negate second-guessing and insure continuity of the investment strategy. The IPS provides a baseline from which to monitor performance of the overall portfolio, as well as the performance of individual money managers. As you know, investment returns and risks are largely determined by the asset allocation decisions. Once decisions are made regarding active versus passive and strategic versus tactical allocation strategies, an appropriate portfolio can be designed for your specific situation. After the portfolio has been implemented, the final critical step is the ongoing monitoring and supervision of the investment process. Your investment advisor should continue to update you regarding fiduciary requirements, maintain performance attribution, recommend terminating managers when appropriate, compute performance calculations, prepare for meeting with you on a quarterly basis and create performance measurement reports.

When seeking financial advice concerning the value of securities or as to the advisability of investing in, purchasing or selling securities, you should know if the person or firm is registered as an investment advisor. Registration at the state or federal level is required if the firm or advisor is providing this advice as part of their business activity for compensation.

Wealth managers and financial planners who have a range of professional designations and licenses are particularly capable of providing comprehensive services. In order to provide a level of service that includes analyzing and planning an individuals investment portfolio, estate plan, retirement plan and tax plan, the firm should be registered as an investment advisor, and have one or more professional designations, such as the CFP® designation (CERTIFIED FINANCIAL PLANNER™ practitioner). Many wealth managers have an area of specialization such as asset management, protection, trusts and estate transfer. As such, it is likely for wealth managers to possess additional licenses, such as Accident, Health and Life insurance licenses for advanced planning services including family security, retirement income, long-term care and estate planning.

Advisors who are dedicated to the profession tend to invest a substantial amount of time building their credentials and are typically committed to ongoing learning and educational requirements.

Recommendations

By far, one of the most effective ways for finding an advisor you can trust is by asking your friends, business associates and other professional advisors for a recommendation. Another option is to contact the Financial Planning Association (FPA) by telephone at

800.322.4237 or by visiting the FPA website at www.fpanet.org for a list of CFP® practitioners in your area. The Financial Planning Association (FPA) is the membership organization for the financial planning community. Its members are dedicated to supporting the financial planning process in order to help people achieve their goals and dreams. FPA believes that everyone needs objective advice to make smart financial decisions and that when seeking the advice of a financial planner, the planner should be a CFP® professional.[4]

Interview Several Practitioners

Most advisors offer a one-hour consultation free of charge to determine if there is a basis upon which to establish a financial planning engagement. This is a great opportunity to ask questions about the firm, the individual advisors and their approach to analyzing and planning a client's investment portfolio. For example, do they utilize a team approach, backed by experts with substantial capability in key areas of investment management and portfolio engineering? Do they adhere to a proven investment process? Request a sample Investment Proposal and Investment Policy Statement (IPS). Ask for information about their background and key areas of specialization. Do they believe in the financial planning process? This is the process of identifying goals, gathering and reviewing financial data and designing and implementing a plan to help you reach your life goals through the proper management of your financial resources. This broad based approach is what distinguishes a CERTIFIED FINANCIAL PLANNER™ practitioner from other advisors who tend to focus on only one aspect of a person's financial life, such as insurance or investments. Ask for a copy of the current firm brochure and the level of services provided. In addition, you can engage in a dialogue about your particular situation describing your need for their services. What do you want to accomplish? Are you interested in establishing a long-term relationship? Are they available to meet with you on a regular basis to assess your progress in relation to your goals and objectives?

Fees and Methods of Compensation

Another matter to discuss with the practitioners you interview is their methods of compensation. How do they charge for the various services they provide? Are they compensated from products purchased, such as investments or insurance? If the only source of compensation that a financial advisor receives is a commission from products purchased, you should be concerned about his or her interest in providing ongoing service in the future. The implementation of a financial plan may or may not require the purchase of products. But with a product driven business model, the emphasis is on transactions that generate commissions. A process driven approach is the preferred way for advisors to provide ongoing service over the years. With this business model, advisors charge a fee based on an hourly rate, flat rate per project, or based on the value of assets under management. With this approach, advisors typically provide ongoing management and financial planning services. Many firms receive both forms of compensation. For example, fees may be charged for the development of written strategic plans for solving specific problems and/or reaching specific goals. There may be a one-time fee for the initial plan development. If you choose to implement the plan, he or she may receive commissions from products purchased, such as insurance or securities.

Prior to the commencement of services, the planner should provide an engagement letter describing the scope of the engagement, the nature of the services to be provided, the form and amount of compensation and copies of all relevant forms at the outset of the financial planning relationship.

Comfort Level

The responsibility for providing financial planning services is a very important relationship between you and your trusted advisor. It is a relationship that typically involves an ongoing exchange of relevant information. Since this relationship is vital to the overall success and achievement of your financial objectives, you should feel confident about the person you choose to work with. You should feel welcome in his and her office. He or she should always be willing to take your call. After all – it is your future!

We Wish You Success

I would like to thank you for reading this book. I hope this year and every year will be a good one for you and your loved ones. While it is hard to say what the future holds, a good financial plan should see you through both good times and bad. The process of building financial security requires a commitment to managing your investments in a way that will enable you to achieve your goals. I hope this book has given you the tools and confidence you need to be successful. By seeking the expertise of a qualified practitioner, as described in this chapter, you will put yourself in the best possible position to achieve your goals and dreams. Once again, thank you for taking the time to read and study this book. It is always an honor and pleasure to help people reach their financial goals. I truly hope that you achieve your goal of financial freedom and security during retirement. Should you have any comments or suggestions, please do not hesitate to contact me – it would be great to hear from you.

Summary

When looking for a financial professional, become familiar with the planners firm, mission, philosophy and beliefs. Is the firm service oriented or product driven?

Look for a planner's dedication to the profession by his or her credentials and a commitment to ongoing educational requirements plus additional hours in specialization, such as retirement, trusts, estate and investment planning.

Most importantly, look for a planner who will put your needs above all else.

References

[1] ING US Financial Services.

[2] ING – Business Journal; Baby Boomers Not Getting the Retirement Message.

[3] Certified Financial Planner Board of Standards, Inc.

[4] Financial Planning Association.

APPENDIX A: For Calculating a Future Value

Periods	2%	3%	4%	5%	6%	7%	8%	9%
1	1.0200	1.0300	1.0400	1.0500	1.0600	1.0700	1.0800	1.0900
2	1.0404	1.0609	1.0816	1.1025	1.1236	1.1449	1.1664	1.1881
3	1.0612	1.0927	1.1249	1.1576	1.1910	1.2250	1.2597	1.2950
4	1.0824	1.1255	1.1699	1.2155	1.2625	1.3108	1.3605	1.4116
5	1.1041	1.1593	1.2167	1.2763	1.3382	1.4026	1.4693	1.5386
6	1.1262	1.1941	1.2653	1.3401	1.4185	1.5007	1.5869	1.6771
7	1.1487	1.2299	1.3159	1.4071	1.5036	1.6058	1.7138	1.8280
8	1.1717	1.2668	1.3686	1.4775	1.5938	1.7182	1.8509	1.9926
9	1.1951	1.3048	1.4233	1.5513	1.6895	1.8385	1.9990	2.1719
10	1.2190	1.3439	1.4802	1.6289	1.7908	1.9672	2.1589	2.3674
11	1.2434	1.3842	1.5395	1.7103	1.8983	2.1049	2.3316	2.5804
12	1.2682	1.4258	1.6010	1.7959	2.0122	2.2522	2.5182	2.8127
13	1.2936	1.4685	1.6651	1.8856	2.1329	2.4098	2.7196	3.0658
14	1.3195	1.5126	1.7317	1.9799	2.2609	2.5785	2.9372	3.3417
15	1.3459	1.5580	1.8009	2.0789	2.3966	2.7590	3.1722	3.6425
16	1.3728	1.6047	1.8730	2.1829	2.5404	2.9522	3.4259	3.9703
17	1.4002	1.6528	1.9479	2.2920	2.6928	3.1588	3.7000	4.3276
18	1.4282	1.7024	2.0258	2.4066	2.8543	3.3799	3.9960	4.7171
19	1.4568	1.7535	2.1068	2.5270	3.0256	3.6165	4.3157	5.1417
20	1.4859	1.8061	2.1911	2.6533	3.2071	3.8697	4.6610	5.6044
21	1.5157	1.8603	2.2788	2.7860	3.3996	4.1406	5.0338	6.1088
22	1.5460	1.9161	2.3699	2.9253	3.6035	4.4304	5.4365	6.6586
23	1.5769	1.9736	2.4647	3.0715	3.8197	4.7405	5.8715	7.2579
24	1.6084	2.0328	2.5633	3.2251	4.0489	5.0724	6.3412	7.9111
25	1.6406	2.0938	2.6658	3.3864	4.2919	5.2474	6.8485	8.6231
26	1.6734	2.1566	2.7725	3.5557	4.5494	5.8074	7.3964	9.3992
27	1.7069	2.2213	2.8834	3.7335	4.8223	6.2139	7.9881	10.2451
28	1.7410	2.2879	2.9987	3.9201	5.1117	6.6488	8.6271	11.1671
29	1.7758	2.3566	3.1187	4.1161	5.4184	7.1143	9.3173	12.1722
30	1.8114	2.4273	3.2434	4.3219	5.7435	7.6123	10.0627	13.2677
31	1.8476	2.5001	3.3731	4.5380	6.0881	8.1451	10.8677	14.4618
32	1.8845	2.5751	3.5081	4.7649	6.4534	8.7153	11.7371	15.7633
33	1.9222	2.6523	3.6484	5.0032	6.8406	9.3253	12.6761	17.1820
34	1.9607	2.7319	3.7943	5.2533	7.2510	9.9781	13.6901	18.7284
35	1.9999	2.8139	3.9461	5.5160	7.6861	10.6766	14.7853	20.4140
36	2.0399	2.8983	4.1039	5.7918	8.1473	11.4239	15.9682	22.2512
37	2.0807	2.9852	4.2681	6.0814	8.6361	12.2236	17.2456	24.2538
38	2.1223	3.0748	4.4388	6.3855	9.1543	13.0793	18.6253	26.4367
39	2.1647	3.1670	4.6164	6.7048	9.7035	13.9948	20.1153	28.8160
40	2.2080	3.2620	4.8010	7.0400	10.2857	14.9745	21.7245	31.4094
41	2.2522	3.3599	4.9931	7.3920	10.9029	16.0227	23.4625	34.2363
42	2.2972	3.4607	5.1928	7.7616	11.5570	17.1443	25.3395	37.3175
43	2.3432	3.5645	5.4005	8.1497	12.2505	18.3444	27.3666	40.6761
44	2.3901	3.6715	5.6165	8.5572	12.9855	19.6285	29.5560	44.3370
45	2.4379	3.7816	5.8412	8.9850	13.7646	21.0025	31.9204	48.3273

APPENDIX B: For Calculating the Lump-Sum Investment Needed to Accumulate a Future Value

Periods	7%	8%	9%	10%	11%	12%
1	1.0000	1.0000	1.0000	1.0000	1.0000	1.0000
2	0.9346	0.9259	0.9174	0.9091	0.9009	0.8929
3	0.8734	0.8573	0.8417	0.8264	0.8116	0.7972
4	0.8163	0.7938	0.7722	0.7513	0.7312	0.7118
5	0.7629	0.7350	0.7084	0.6830	0.6587	0.6355
6	0.7130	0.6806	0.6499	0.6209	0.5935	0.5674
7	0.6663	0.6302	0.5963	0.5645	0.5346	0.5066
8	0.6228	0.5835	0.5470	0.5132	0.4817	0.4523
9	0.5820	0.5403	0.5019	0.4665	0.4339	0.4039
10	0.5439	0.5002	0.4604	0.4241	0.3909	0.3606
11	0.5083	0.4632	0.4224	0.3855	0.3522	0.3220
12	0.4751	0.4289	0.3875	0.3505	0.3173	0.2875
13	0.4440	0.3971	0.3555	0.3186	0.2858	0.2567
14	0.4150	0.3677	0.3262	0.2897	0.2575	0.2292
15	0.3878	0.3405	0.2992	0.2633	0.2320	0.2046
16	0.3624	0.3152	0.2745	0.2394	0.2090	0.1827
17	0.3387	0.2919	0.2519	0.2176	0.1883	0.1631
18	0.3166	0.2703	0.2311	0.1978	0.1696	0.1456
19	0.2959	0.2502	0.2120	0.1799	0.1528	0.1300
20	0.2765	0.2317	0.1945	0.1635	0.1377	0.1161
21	0.2584	0.2145	0.1784	0.1486	0.1240	0.1037
22	0.2415	0.1987	0.1637	0.1351	0.1117	0.0926
23	0.2257	0.1839	0.1502	0.1228	0.1007	0.0826
24	0.2109	0.1703	0.1378	0.1117	0.0907	0.0738
25	0.1971	0.1577	0.1264	0.1015	0.0817	0.0659
26	0.1842	0.1460	0.1160	0.0923	0.0736	0.0588
27	0.1722	0.1352	0.1064	0.0839	0.0663	0.0525
28	0.1609	0.1252	0.0976	0.0763	0.0597	0.0469
29	0.1504	0.1159	0.0895	0.0693	0.0538	0.0419
30	0.1406	0.1073	0.0822	0.0630	0.0485	0.0374
31	0.1314	0.0944	0.0754	0.0573	0.0437	0.0334
32	0.1228	0.0920	0.0691	0.0521	0.0394	0.0298
33	0.1147	0.0852	0.0634	0.0474	0.0355	0.0266
34	0.1072	0.0789	0.0582	0.0431	0.0319	0.0238
35	0.1002	0.0730	0.0534	0.0391	0.0288	0.0212
36	0.0937	0.0676	0.0490	0.0356	0.0259	0.0189
37	0.0875	0.0626	0.0449	0.0323	0.0234	0.0169
38	0.0818	0.0580	0.0412	0.0294	0.0210	0.0151
39	0.0765	0.0537	0.0378	0.0267	0.0190	0.0135
40	0.0715	0.0497	0.0347	0.0243	0.0171	0.0120

APPENDIX C: For Calculating the Periodic Investment Needed to Accumulate a Future Value

Future Value Factors

Periods	6%	7%	8%	9%	10%	11%	12%
1	1.0000	1.0000	1.0000	1.0000	1.0000	1.0000	1.0000
2	2.0600	2.0700	2.0800	2.0900	2.1000	2.1100	2.1200
3	3.1836	3.2149	3.2464	3.2781	3.3100	3.3421	3.3744
4	4.3746	4.4399	4.5061	4.5731	4.6410	4.7097	4.7793
5	5.6371	5.7507	5.8666	5.9847	6.1051	6.2278	6.3528
6	6.9753	7.1533	7.3359	7.5233	7.7156	7.9129	8.1152
7	8.3938	8.6540	8.9228	9.2004	9.4872	9.7833	10.0890
8	9.8975	10.2598	10.6366	11.0285	11.4359	11.8594	12.2997
9	11.4913	11.9780	12.4876	13.0210	13.5795	14.1640	14.7757
10	13.1808	13.8164	14.4866	15.1929	15.9374	16.7220	17.5487
11	14.9716	15.7836	16.6455	17.5603	18.5312	19.5614	20.6546
12	16.8699	17.8885	18.9771	20.1407	21.3843	22.7132	24.1331
13	18.8821	20.1406	21.4953	22.9534	24.5227	26.2116	28.0291
14	21.0151	22.5505	24.2149	26.0192	27.9750	30.0949	32.3926
15	23.2760	25.1290	27.1521	29.3609	31.7725	34.4054	37.2797
16	25.6725	27.8881	30.3243	33.0034	35.9497	39.1899	42.7533
17	28.2129	30.8402	33.7502	36.9737	40.5447	44.5008	48.8837
18	30.9057	33.9990	37.4502	41.3013	45.5992	50.3959	55.7497
19	33.7600	37.3790	41.4463	46.0185	51.1591	56.9395	63.4397
20	36.7856	40.9955	45.7620	51.1601	57.2750	64.2028	72.0524
21	39.9927	44.8652	50.4229	56.7645	64.0025	72.2651	81.6987
22	43.3923	49.0057	55.4568	62.8733	71.4027	81.2143	92.5026
23	46.9958	53.4361	60.8933	69.5319	79.5430	91.1479	104.6029
24	50.8156	58.1767	66.7648	76.7898	88.4973	102.1742	118.1552
25	54.8645	63.2490	73.1059	84.7009	98.3471	114.4133	133.3339
26	59.1564	68.6765	79.9544	93.3240	109.1818	127.9988	150.3339
27	63.7058	74.4838	87.3508	102.7231	121.0999	143.0786	169.3740
28	68.5281	80.6977	95.3388	112.9682	134.2099	159.8173	190.6989
29	73.6398	87.3465	103.9659	124.1354	148.6309	178.3972	214.5825
30	79.0582	94.4608	113.2832	136.3075	164.4940	199.0209	241.3327
31	84.8017	102.0730	123.3459	149.5752	181.9434	221.9132	271.2926
32	90.8898	110.2182	134.2135	164.0370	201.1378	247.3236	304.8477
33	97.3432	118.9334	145.9506	179.8003	222.2515	275.5292	342.4294
34	104.1838	128.2588	158.6267	196.9823	245.4767	306.8374	384.5210
35	111.4348	138.2369	172.3168	215.7108	271.0244	341.5896	431.6635
36	119.1209	148.9135	187.1021	236.1247	299.1268	380.1644	484.4631
37	127.2681	160.3374	203.0703	258.3759	330.0395	422.9825	543.5987
38	135.9042	172.5610	220.3159	282.6298	364.0434	470.5106	609.8305
39	145.0585	185.6403	238.9412	309.0665	401.4478	523.2667	684.0102
40	154.7620	199.6351	259.0565	337.8824	442.5926	581.8261	767.0914

APPENDIX D: For Tabulating Future Values

Year	Annual Income ($_____X Future Value Factor)	Year	Annual Income ($_____X Future Value Factor)
1	$_____	26	$_____
2	$_____	27	$_____
3	$_____	28	$_____
4	$_____	29	$_____
5	$_____	30	$_____
6	$_____	31	$_____
7	$_____	32	$_____
8	$_____	33	$_____
9	$_____	34	$_____
10	$_____	35	$_____
11	$_____	36	$_____
12	$_____	37	$_____
13	$_____	38	$_____
14	$_____	39	$_____
15	$_____	40	$_____
16	$_____	41	$_____
17	$_____	42	$_____
18	$_____	43	$_____
19	$_____	44	$_____
20	$_____	45	$_____
21	$_____	46	$_____
22	$_____	47	$_____
23	$_____	48	$_____
24	$_____	49	$_____
25	$_____	50	$_____

APPENDIX E: For Tabulating the Lump-Sum Investment Needed to Provide an Inflation-Adjusted Income

Year	Annual Income (_____X Future Value Factor)	Discounted Value (_____X Present Value Factor)	Year	Annual Income (_____X Future Value Factor)	Discounted Value (_____X Present Value Factor)
1	$_____	$_____	26	$_____	$_____
2	$_____	$_____	27	$_____	$_____
3	$_____	$_____	28	$_____	$_____
4	$_____	$_____	29	$_____	$_____
5	$_____	$_____	30	$_____	$_____
6	$_____	$_____	31	$_____	$_____
7	$_____	$_____	32	$_____	$_____
8	$_____	$_____	33	$_____	$_____
9	$_____	$_____	34	$_____	$_____
10	$_____	$_____	35	$_____	$_____
11	$_____	$_____	36	$_____	$_____
12	$_____	$_____	37	$_____	$_____
13	$_____	$_____	38	$_____	$_____
14	$_____	$_____	39	$_____	$_____
15	$_____	$_____	40	$_____	$_____
16	$_____	$_____	41	$_____	$_____
17	$_____	$_____	42	$_____	$_____
18	$_____	$_____	43	$_____	$_____
19	$_____	$_____	44	$_____	$_____
20	$_____	$_____	45	$_____	$_____
21	$_____	$_____	46	$_____	$_____
22	$_____	$_____	47	$_____	$_____
23	$_____	$_____	48	$_____	$_____
24	$_____	$_____	49	$_____	$_____
25	$_____	$_____	50	$_____	$_____
	Total	$_____		Total	$_____

APPENDIX F:

ESTATE TAX BALANCE SHEET

ASSETS	Assets titled in own name	Assets titled in spouses name	Assets titled jointly	Assets transferred by beneficiary designation	Total Assets
Cash/Cash Equivalents	$_____	$_____	$_____	$_____	$_____
Money Market Instruments	$_____	$_____	$_____	$_____	$_____
Annuities & Fixed Income Securities	$_____	$_____	$_____	$_____	$_____
Investments					
Common Stocks	$_____	$_____	$_____	$_____	$_____
Mutual Funds	$_____	$_____	$_____	$_____	$_____
Options, Commodities & Collectibles	$_____	$_____	$_____	$_____	$_____
Royalties & Mineral Interests	$_____	$_____	$_____	$_____	$_____
Other Investments	$_____	$_____	$_____	$_____	$_____
Retirement Plans					
	$_____	$_____	$_____	$_____	$_____
	$_____	$_____	$_____	$_____	$_____
	$_____	$_____	$_____	$_____	$_____
Qualified Plans					
	$_____	$_____	$_____	$_____	$_____
	$_____	$_____	$_____	$_____	$_____
IRA's					
	$_____	$_____	$_____	$_____	$_____
	$_____	$_____	$_____	$_____	$_____
	$_____	$_____	$_____	$_____	$_____
Closely Held Business Interest(s)	$_____	$_____	$_____	$_____	$_____
	$_____	$_____	$_____	$_____	$_____
Real Estate					
Personal Residence	$_____	$_____	$_____	$_____	$_____
Vacation Home	$_____	$_____	$_____	$_____	$_____
Personal Property					
Household Contents	$_____	$_____	$_____	$_____	$_____
Automobiles	$_____	$_____	$_____	$_____	$_____
Jewelry & Collectables	$_____	$_____	$_____	$_____	$_____
Other Personal Property	$_____	$_____	$_____	$_____	$_____
Notes Receivable	$_____	$_____	$_____	$_____	$_____
Totals	$_____	$_____	$_____	$_____	$_____

APPENDIX G:

Uniform Distribution Table

Age of IRA Owner OR Plan Participant	Life Expectancy (in years)	Age of IRA Owner OR Plan Participant	Life Expectancy (in years)
70	27.4	93	9.6
71	26.5	94	9.1
72	25.6	95	8.6
73	24.7	96	8.1
74	23.8	97	7.6
75	22.9	98	7.1
76	22.0	99	6.7
77	21.2	100	6.3
78	20.3	101	5.9
79	19.5	102	5.5
80	18.7	103	5.2
81	17.9	104	4.9
82	17.1	105	4.5
83	16.3	106	4.2
84	15.5	107	3.9
85	14.8	108	3.7
86	14.1	109	3.4
87	13.4	110	3.1
88	12.7	111	2.9
89	12.0	112	2.6
90	11.4	113	2.4
91	10.8	114	2.1
92	10.2	115	1.9

APPENDIX H:

2006 Tax Rate Schedule

Taxable Income ($)	Base Amount Of Tax ($)	Plus	Rate On Excess (%) (also called marginal tax rate or tax bracket)	Of the Amount Over ($)
Married filing jointly and surviving spouses				
0 to 15,100	0.00	plus	10	0
15,100 to 61,300	1,510.00	plus	15	15,100
61,300 to 123,700	8,440.00	plus	25	61,300
123,700 to 188,450	24,040.00	plus	28	123,700
188,450 to 336,550	42,170.00	plus	33	188,450
Over 336,550	91,043.00	plus	35	336,550
Single				
0 to 7,550	0.00	plus	10	0
7,550 to 30,650	755.00	plus	15	7,550
30,650 to 74,200	4,220.00	plus	25	30,650
74,200 to 154,800	15,107.50	plus	28	74,200
154,800 to 336,550	37,675.50	plus	33	154,800
Over 336,550	97,653.00	plus	35	336,550
Head of household				
0 to 10,750	0.00	plus	10	0
10,750 to 41,050	1,075.00	plus	15	10,750
41,050 to 106,000	5,620.00	plus	25	41,050
106,000 to 171,650	21,857.50	plus	28	106,000
171,650 to 336,550	40,239.50	plus	33	171,650
Over 336,550	94,656.50	plus	35	336,550
Married filing separately				
0 to 7,550	0.00	plus	10	0
7,550 to 30,650	755.00	plus	15	7,550
30,650 to 61,850	4,220.00	plus	25	30,650
61,850 to 94,225	12,020.00	plus	28	61,850
94,225, to 168,275	21,085.00	plus	33	94,225
Over 168,275	45,521.50	plus	35	168,275
Estates and Trusts				
0 to 2,050	0.00	plus	15	0
2,050 to 4,850	307.50	plus	25	2,050
4,850 to 7,400	1,007.50	plus	28	4,850
7,400 to 10,050	1,721.50	plus	33	7,400
Over 10,050	2,596.00	plus	35	10,050

Source: 2006 Federal Tax Rate Schedules, IRS; 2006 Federal Tax Rates for Estates and Trusts

Index

Printed in the United States
207619BV00002B/91-102/A